The Cost of Christian Living

Currency in kingdom life

MARTYN PERCY

BRF
Ministries

'Martyn is not in thrall to anyone except God and he is quite brilliantly articulate, biblically literate and anchored in the struggle of actual living… With much courage he discusses currency, money and debt.'
Iain Torrance, president emeritus of Princeton Theological Seminary

'You will find much you thought you understood stood on its head by Percy's determined "monetising" of biblical material – because to his eyes the myriad references to money matters are already there, if only we let ourselves look.'
Peter Selby, formerly bishop of Worcester, author of *An Idol Unmasked*

'This book is a challenging read for any Christian. Based on deep scholarship and vividly written, it helps us bridge the centuries and imagine afresh the real flesh-and-blood Jesus and his uncomfortable message.'
Stephen Green, BRF Ministries' vice president and former group chief executive of HSBC

'Percy uses biblical stories… to explore the intersection of faith and finance. This book is a timely call to readers and the church to embrace God's radical, abundant love for a truly inclusive kingdom.'
Jeremy Greaves, archbishop of Brisbane

'This inspiring and moving book maps new spaces for theological thinking on the nature of God's kingdom currency… Martyn brings readers constructively beyond their accepted way, engaging their understanding, ideas and patterns of thought.'
Paul Kwong, archbishop emeritus, Hong Kong

'This book will not only change your thinking about money – it may even change your thinking about God's church.'
Mark Edington, bishop in charge, The Convocation of Episcopal Churches in Europe

'Percy's accessible writing and profound theological reflections inspire a renewed understanding of Christian discipleship, rooted in love, service and the abundant grace of God.'
The Very Revd Dr Isaac Pooblan, provost of St Andrew's Cathedral, Aberdeen

BRF Ministries

15 The Chambers, Vineyard
Abingdon OX14 3FE
+44 (0)1865 319700 | brf.org.uk

Bible Reading Fellowship (BRF) is a charity (233280) and company limited by
guarantee (301324), registered in England and Wales

EU Authorised Representative: Easy Access System Europe – Mustamäe tee 50,
10621 Tallinn, Estonia, gpsr.requests@easproject.com

ISBN 978 1 80039 349 3
First published 2025
All rights reserved

Contents

Foreword 7

Beginnings: Stewards of kingdom currency 12

PART 1: MISSION, MINISTRY, MONEY

1 Two sides of the same coin 25

2 Money magic 35

3 Rewards and bonuses 44

4 Economic miracles 55

5 Crumbs of comfort 65

6 Tax returns 75

Interlude: The gospel according to Rembrandt, Frank Baum and
Elton John 85

PART 2: COUNTING THE COST

7 Bureau de change 97

8 The price of oil 106

9 The currency of love 115

10 Thirty pieces of silver 125

11 Gambling at the foot of the cross 134

12 Burial costs 143

Endings: Mutuality and building society 153

Discussion questions 162

Appendix I: Costing salvation – Ignatian exercises 168

Appendix II: Coins and currency in the New Testament 170

Appendix III: Additional online resources 173

Notes 174

Foreword

It was several conversations at the 2022 *Church Times* Preaching Festival that first ignited the spark for this book, and I am hugely grateful to those who pressed their questions and helped refine my thinking on the nature of God's 'kingdom currency'. As with my previous book of meditations published by BRF Ministries (*An Advent Manifesto*, 2023), I am upfront about my biblical knowledge and exegetical skills. I am not a professional biblical scholar. I am more towards the Bible-busker end of the spectrum rather than the symphony concert standard. This is honesty on my part, not false humility.

The Cost of Christian Living: Currency in kingdom life is written for individuals and study groups keen to wrestle with thematic issues in the gospels that would otherwise remain unattended to. It draws on other conversations too, especially with Anglican-Episcopalian congregations, clergy and students in Hong Kong (where I am privileged to serve as provost theologian at Ming Hua Theological College), Macao (at the University of Saint Joseph, where I also lecture), the Convocation of Episcopal Churches in Europe (the American congregations) and St Andrew's Cathedral in Aberdeen, Scotland. I owe them a real debt of gratitude.

I am also profoundly grateful to friends and colleagues at Virginia Theological Seminary for their willingness to share some of their journey on slavery reparation. Their testimony represents an inspiring witness to the possibility of kingdom life in the here and now. I particularly want to express my gratitude to members of the congregation at St John's Cathedral Hong Kong, Dr Janice Tsang and Dr Ting Kin Cheung, for their friendship, fellowship, conversation, company and care as this book has taken shape. Likewise, appreciation and gratitude are due to the dean of the cathedral, Kwok Keung Chan, and many others within the remarkable congregations of Hong Kong Sheng Kung Hui, where mission and ministry prioritise significant programmes of social welfare intervention and wide-ranging educational endeavour. I thank them all enormously.

As will be apparent, I have divided the book into two parts, each with six chapters, which can work for group discussions and Bible studies. Part 1 (Mission, ministry, money) will work for study groups and individuals for almost any time in the Christian year. Part 2 (Counting the cost) is geared more for Lent, Holy Week and Easter and leans into the gospel narratives that are traditionally concerned with the events of that period in the Christian calendar. We also take some of the stories from the gospels that are concerned with money and lead to the arrest, betrayal, crucifixion and burial of Jesus.

There is an interlude provided between parts 1 and 2, which also serves to underscore a theme of the book that dwells on how churches are to be inclusive and incorporative bodies. Here, one of the central narratives in the gospels, the parable of the prodigal son, is interpreted in keeping with the themes of money, currency and value. In the final section, after the reflections, there are some resources to help individuals and groups navigate their way through some of the issues that the book raises, and they might also assist with new readings of the gospels.

Concepts of currency and value are laden in the gospels within stories of bread, wine, hunger, feasting, famine and friendship. The parables and miracles of Jesus, and the stories of encounters with him, all point to questions of worth, debt and redemption. The Bible speaks of redemption in terms of purchase, with God paying any price for his people. Any discussion of money belongs to the broader and deeper gospel ecology of value and currency, for we are all given God's love freely and taken out of the bondage of debt. Christian stewardship is taking care of God's eternal, limitless resources. It is also about ensuring that the treasure of heaven is made available for all.

Money is merely a means to an end for the kingdom of God. That is why our treatment of currency in this book is intentionally broad. Any economy is about far more than money. It is about sharing, compassion, fairness, justice, mercy and truth. While money plays a very significant role in the lives of people all over the world, each and every day, food itself is also a currency. Indeed, in economies where there is no money (as in ancient times, but still witnessed in remote tribes today), food, goods and services are exchanged. Such things have real value as currency.

In the gospels, food, crop and harvest stories are essential for understanding the kingdom of God. That is why Jesus' teaching on growth and mission is so careful. Some seeds work in one kind of soil, but don't necessarily fare well in every kind of ground. Some are given grounds to toil in terms of mission which are stony, hard and unyielding. To others, the ground is soft and fertile, and to others, the competition of weeds and the hunger of the birds means that all growth is quickly snatched away. Jesus' teaching on the ecology of the kingdom of God was always an invitation to take part in levelling off the ground around us and to take collective responsibility for those who have less, or perhaps nothing. God's provision is for sharing with others, not hoarding for ourselves.

Today, our language for food is inherently politicised. 'Food banks' are perhaps the best example of this. They do exceptional work, for sure – and have become a staple necessity in harsh and unforgiving economic times. Yet the word 'bank' borrows from the world of monetarism, and indeed, that very monetarism might be said to be partly responsible for the existence of food banks. Banks lend but they do not give. So how do we talk about money, the love of which is one root cause of another person's poverty? Our language for that shapes our thinking about money, which is so ancient and ingrained that we rarely think about it. How did we ever come to talk about 'owning shares', when sharing is not about ownership?

This makes 'food bank' a rather ambivalent term. Those for whom money is secure will find the idea of a bank reassuring. It keeps money and investments secure, manages what you have, and may even pay interest. For those in debt, however, banks can be places of pain, regret and remorse, summoning memories of repossession, unaffordable loans and the stigma of losing control of one's finances. Food aid and bank become intertwined, adding guilt to any stigma already there. Terms like 'larder', 'hub', 'store' and 'pantry' would convey something quite different to those in need, and to those who were donating or supporting such ventures.

Please note, and for the avoidance of doubt, this book is *not* written for churches wanting to increase their giving to themselves, their denomination or their diocese. Indeed, if you bought it for that purpose, you might want to give the book to someone else. This is very much written for churches and congregations who want to explore how to make outward and external investments in their communities and make a far more profound impact in their world.

Mission and ministry are not for the benefit of the church. It is Jesus' lavish expenditure of love for those who have not found justice, healing, mercy and grace in this life. The church is only meant to be God's agency for this. We measure our authenticity not by recruitment but by how much we can give away. The scriptures teach us that the vast majority of recipients of free, unmerited grace may not ever thank us for such help and support, much less join in the tireless work of self-giving love.

Such is the nature of God's economy. It is, at its best, simultaneously abundant (endlessly) and yet bankrupt. Not for nothing is the parable of the manna in the desert a word to the wise (Exodus 16). God's love cannot be hoarded. Whatever you may have, share it with others. Today.

To be sure, many churches and denominations in our time are fretful and fearful for their futures. Some grasp for growth; others hunger for success; and others hole up and hunker down, hoping this era will pass and they will somehow survive. I have written this book against such hubristic conceits, and it is centred in a different place.

The Cost of Christian Living is only a tiny contribution to that agenda. But sometimes, small change makes all the difference. If these reflections persuade you to reinvest in building the kingdom of God here and now, there is still hope for the currency we know as 'Christian life' within our cultures. On such, God still pays handsome interest – and there are dividends. But your investment and deposit are required if this work is ever to begin.

Martyn Percy

Beginnings:
Stewards of kingdom currency

This anecdote, though possibly fictional, conveys a profound truth. The American tycoon John D. Rockefeller was once asked: 'How much wealth is enough for happiness?' His purported response was: 'Just a little more.' This raises a crucial question: when does wealth become excessive? We often witness the juxtaposition of ostentatious affluence and abject poverty. The opulent and the destitute are often neighbours. Vast riches and reserves overlook a world of unending scarcity and distressing dearth.

Yet we rarely discuss money. In many cultures, it is considered impolite, brash or too personal. Like politics and religion, there are unspoken rules that keep money off the table, even among friends. Money talk is for professionals, industry, bankers, couples and families to navigate. In our churches, the topic is cautiously approached and heavily veiled in the rhetoric that emphasises support, stewardship, ministry, contribution and the like. As one preacher observed, money is a commodity that people relentlessly pursue six days a week and then prefer not to discuss on Sunday.

This book offers a fresh perspective on the topic of money – or currency – in the gospels. We will delve into the ways in which money is woven into parables, miracles and encounters. However, our primary focus is on currency – the tangible representations of value we exchange for our needs and desires.

Money, in various forms, has played a significant role in human history for millennia. The English term 'money' is derived from the Latin word *moneta*, which originally referred to a mint that produced coinage.

Going further back, Moneta was a title of the ancient Roman goddess Juno or Hera for the ancient Greeks. She was the goddess of childbirth, marriage and counsel, ensuring the stability of the state. Her shrines and temples across the ancient world were responsible for minting and issuing coinage. But *moneta* had other meanings as well. It also signified to warn, advise and admonish. The word 'monitor' is a direct descendant of this term.

Currency is something else. It comes from the Latin root *currens*, which refers to the condition of flowing and of keeping things running. In ancient societies without the means to coin money, complex systems of bartering evolved. That might be so much wheat for one chicken or bales of straw in return for fruit. Such economies were well-established in ancient Britain, along with rules and guidelines for equivalence and exchange. I have a friend, an anthropologist, who researched tribal Pentecostalism in a remote part of Papua New Guinea where the currency was pig's teeth. A main feature of the diet, perhaps unsurprisingly, was pork.

Bartering economies feature in the Old Testament. 'Eye for eye, tooth for tooth' (Exodus 21:23–27) is an obvious example and establishes the principle of reciprocity in justice. Monetary compensation was not an option: it was a case of measure for measure, as Shakespeare noted. Long before the Old Testament, the Babylonian Code of Hammurabi set out the terms of reciprocity and equivalence. If a person kills another person, the only penalty is death.

So, many currencies don't involve money at all, at least directly. As the poet U.A. Fanthorpe suggested, love is a kind of currency.[1] Mutual trust and respect are currencies; they must flow both ways for the currency to have any value. Kindness is a currency; arguably, our entire human and social economy depends on it.

Currency is the main concern of this book, but we will be drawing on several of Jesus' encounters, parables and miracles. That means, of course, that we must attend to the motifs of debt, payment, purchase and sacrifice that are inevitably a kind of currency in the New Testament. Put simply, what was owed to God? Who was paying? What debts were cleared, by whom and how? What returns are required? The cost of Christian living is one of expenditure and accrual, of giving away and gaining.

Jesus' kingdom of God project was a serious reset, if not a full-blown revolution of economy and currency and how we think of *value*. Jesus forever teased his audiences with exaggerated and sometimes absurd economies of scale. Who would leave 99 sheep (worth a lot of money) to find just one? Wise and experienced shepherds would write off the missing one. Who, seriously, would count the number of hairs on your head?

Jesus' preaching, practice, miracles and ministry placed enormous value on those who were undervalued, devalued or regarded as value-less. At the same time, Jesus consistently challenged those who held misplaced values, overestimated their own value while undervaluing others or prevented people from discovering their true value. The currency of Jesus' kingdom of God project is centred on the flow of God's love, grace, mercy, kindness and tenderness.

Jesus embodies and teaches that this kingdom cannot be bankrupt and that its resources, assets, treasures and wealth are imperishable, limitless and free. So Jesus opposes those who apply tariffs and restrictions on God's kingdom currency. Jesus chides those who seek to profit from it or restrict access to God's abundant funds of love and grace, which are free. Jesus says you cannot earn or deserve the gift, but you can do the will of God by sharing what you have been given.

The gospels are full of references to coins, money, taxes, costs, pricing, wages, bribery and gambling. Yet money has no life of its own. In the right hands, it can do a great deal of good. In the wrong hands, it may do nothing or even cause harm. Jesus warns about this when he states how difficult it is 'for a rich person to enter the kingdom of God' (Mark 10:25). The problem is not so much money as what consumes the possessor and what they value. Jesus knew his Old Testament here:

> He who loves money will not be satisfied with money, nor he who loves wealth with his income; this also is vanity… As he came from his mother's womb he shall go again, naked as he came, and shall take nothing for his toil that he may carry away in his hand.
> ECCLESIASTES 5:10, 15

Money is *not* 'the root of all evil'. The scriptures say that 'the love of money is a root of all kinds of evils' (1 Timothy 6:10). This is the whole point of Jesus' parable of the rich fool. The person who places his confidence and finds his joy in material wealth has a false sense of security and happiness. Such a person is in for a rude awakening when the final summons beckons. 'Fool! This night your soul is required of you, and the things you have prepared, whose will they be?' (Luke 12:20). Death is the great equaliser.

Mark's parable of the 'watchful servants' (13:32–37) is not just a condensed version of Matthew's parable (25:1–13) of the wise and foolish virgins. It's a more nuanced narrative, yet it echoes one of the constant themes in Jesus' teachings, stressing the imminent arrival of the kingdom. The imagery vividly portrays a master who could appear at any moment, expecting to find the servants prepared and everything in order, thereby emphasising the importance of readiness.

Like so many of the parables of this kind – here we have a banquet, invitations and so forth, but also a rallying call to 'be ready' – they seek to remind us that all that we have is ultimately God's; that what we are about to be involved in does not belong to us. We are guests of God at his table, not the caterers. We run to his timetable; we must simply be ready.

The parable connects to the advice that Luke offers just before his account: prepare – make purses that don't wear out (Luke 12:33–34). Always make yourself ready. Meanwhile, in Mark's gospel, the parable of the watchful slaves is preceded by that of the faithful or fruitful fig tree, and there are more calls to watch for signs and be alert.

Stewardship is not just a role; it's a responsibility. It's about being prepared to welcome our master and to handle all that has been entrusted to us with care. This is not a call to passivity; the servant must manage the household diligently. They are not required to stay awake all night but to be ready to respond when the knock comes and to demonstrate good order and management. However, they must remember that everything ultimately belongs to the master. The master is not to be feared but respected, underscoring the weight of responsibility in stewardship.

We encounter similar themes in the parable that follows the wise and foolish virgins in Matthew 25 – the parable of the talents. This is a story about stewardship and wise investment. It is a cautionary tale about the consequences of not even attempting to invest or choosing to hoard out of fear, insecurity and selfishness. The three servants are each entrusted with money by their master before he departs for an extended period. One receives five talents, another two, and the other is given one, highlighting the importance of faith and selflessness in stewardship.

We are not told why the division is uneven; it is easy to imagine good reasons based on age, experience and aptitude. It may have something to do with ability and agency. However, each recipient has something in common: a gift they must return. The gift comes with an expectation of work, investment and interest and returns.

Each servant is entrusted with some of the master's money, and two make the most of this opportunity by thinking about how the money can be used to earn even more. But one is uncertain of the whole enterprise and buries what he has been given. Eventually, the master returns and the servants are called to account. The first two are proud of their endeavours; they have used what they had well and return double to their master. He is delighted, and each is praised for being faithful over a little and promised that he will be entrusted with a lot more. So far, so good.

However, the last servant is somewhat self-righteous about their own indecision. There is a certain posturing and even justification for inaction: 'I knew you to be a mean and unfair master,' they reason, 'and I was afraid, so I hid the talent, and here it is returned just as it was given.'

The master is far from impressed. Even if he can be considered a hard master, the servant could at least have earned some interest in the money (this is quite a sneering comment as usury was forbidden). Instead, the servant rejects the gift and opportunity given; the sum is returned unused. Fear and mistrust paralysed the last servant. The ending is harsh. The one who didn't try has the gift he didn't ask for handed to someone else. The servant is dismissed into the darkness.

The same kinds of dynamics are at work in Luke's parable of the ten minas (19:11–27; 'minas' is sometimes rendered as 'pounds'). This time, ten servants receive ten minas – one each. The master (or nobleman) leaves for a far country and instructs the servants plainly, 'Engage in business until I come' (v. 13). When that day eventually arrives, he calls the servants to give an account of how they have traded. There are three recorded replies.

The first made ten minas from the one they were given, and their reward is to be given charge over ten cities. A second made five minas and receives custody of five cities for their labour. But the third – out of fear, we are told – kept the mina safe in a napkin and did nothing. The servant is admonished for not investing the mina even in the bank. Despite protests, the mina is promptly confiscated and given to the one with ten.

The coinage in these parables is a cypher for the most valued things of the kingdom of God and, by implication, the church's treasures. The most valuable treasures here do not, I think, have much to do with money, at least directly. The treasures are values of the kingdom, which are the fruit of the Spirit (Galatians 5:22–23) and the sixfold gifts of the Spirit (listed in Isaiah 11:1–2): wisdom, understanding, counsel, might, knowledge and fear of the Lord. Perhaps this should be obvious, but it is still worth stating: the church has nothing else to trade with. Christ's kingdom currency is cashless, yet priceless. God's currency is love. It flows from God. Constantly.

The implications for churches are radical. Empty your safes and bank accounts and put the money to God's work. Love, imagination, preparedness and resolve are at the heart of faithful and authentic stewardship, as is the willingness to take risks. Hoarding out of fear or playing it safe is admonished. It is not our money to keep. The church will not be thanked or rewarded for a healthy balance sheet.

These three parables of Jesus (watchful servants, talents and minas) push in the same direction. They are a radical call to take seriously how we live in our world, conscious that we will all at some point be called to account for how we have cared for and responded to all that God has given us and called us to. As a teenager, I was often told to keep short accounts with God: don't delay making things right. The parables are a call to expansive, eager, righteous and risky living. We must consciously think about what that means for us in the different spheres of our lives, for others who ache and long for a truly human life and for the life of the world around us.

These days, many denominational, congregational and diocesan narratives about stewardship are unintentionally framed around the servant who fails to take a risk and does not invest. Put more starkly, if the goal of stewardship is just to keep the church going, then there will be little interest and few returns (pun intended). So how can we do our best to be sure that we are living our Christian lives, not in terms of our survival or perhaps long-term security, but in terms of the things Christ is calling us to right here and now?

First, the urgency of Jesus' words suggests that we must seek him in the lonely, the persecuted, the hungry, the scorned and the victimised. This is no easy task, but it is fundamental. We are first and foremost to seek Christ in the people and places that the world habitually rejects or oppresses. In loving the unloved and unseen, we begin to meet our maker.

Second, grace takes many forms. Jesus often talks in his parable about noticing, feeding and visiting – simple things. We sometimes need to look for very clear forms of service among ourselves and others. The gospel's heart is set on raising up the fallen, the shunned and the oppressed.

Third, we remember that true religion is love, not reward. In giving, we receive; in dying, we are born; love is all there is. One of the rich ironies of our faith is that it is for others; rather like our church – it is the only club that exists for non-members. A parish church is the inside place for outsiders, the place of belonging to those who have nowhere to belong.

The Christian vocation remains compellingly simple: to be like Christ, to love one another as he loves us and in the same heartbeat to love those who have no one to love them. Jesus says, 'Truly, I say to you, as you did it to one of the least of these… you did it to me' (Matthew 25:40). We are to serve the least in the world – just as Christ does. God has invested in us to do this with his free love.

During the time I was writing this, it was hard not to draw some inferences from the parables on stewardship with the current attempts of the Church of England to establish a fund of reparation in relation to their role in the Atlantic slave trade. It is undeniable that the present wealth of many denominations and institutions in Britain had profits and derivatives from slavery baked into their endowment.

The Church of England recently announced the creation of a £100 million fund as a gesture towards reparation. It has also conceded that the fund should be more like £1 billion, though it is unclear from whom or where the remaining £900 million would come from. To be clear, the offer is not to give away either £100 million or £1 billion. It is, rather, to operate a fund from inside the Church of England that would pay out support based on annual interest.

On the face it, this might seem like good stewardship. But I dissent. The money came to the church through slavery and is being retained by the same church, who will then decide on the proportionate causes they deem might benefit. There are few signs of genuine remorse, reparation and change. When one does come across them, however, they shine out as exemplary. Virginia Theological Seminary, near Washington DC, was for much of the 19th century more associated with Confederate sympathies than support for the Union. On the day the American Civil War broke out, contemporary accounts record some students and faculty leaving their desks, books still unfinished and signing up to fight for the south.

In preparation for its bicentenary in 2023, Virginia Theological Seminary commissioned a study of its history in respect of slavery. As it turned out, the seminary had never owned slaves, at least directly. But it had employed them, or rather used them for labour, since local slaveowners had hired them out to the seminary for labour during summer and winter breaks. And, of course, it was the slaveowners who were remunerated, not the workers. A number of the early benefactors of the seminary were slave-owners. All of this was hiding in plain sight in the small classified advertisements of the newspapers from the time.

To the great credit of the seminary and its Dean, the Very Revd Dr Ian Markham, the initiative for reparation was unique, ground-breaking and generative. Many of the living ancestors of the enslaved were traced. They are now being paid a modest annual annuity by the seminary, in perpetuity. Furthermore, they have been made incorporated members of the seminary and can dine there and use the facilities for free and as equals.

For some descendants, still living in the area and who were contacted through this initiative, this was a painful reminder of their enslaved ancestors, only a few generations apart. It also reminded many of the painful journey over the last few centuries to secure equality. There was a segregated seminary for black students that ran from 1878 to 1951. Only very slowly has progressiveness become proactive not reactive.

There can be no authentic change without a reckoning that our wider culture was (and still is) structurally racist. Slavery and forced indentured labour were crimes against humanity, an affront to human dignity and basic human rights, and a blasphemy against God. It is only because the truth of this history has been faced, owned and repented of that Markham's reparation initiative could move forward. It avowedly testifies to a basic gospel principle, namely giving all people freedom to self-determine in the here and now, and not to dictate how a sinful past and its current legacy should be atoned for. As an act of reparation and compassion, this was a revolutionary act of stewardship.

Therefore, protecting or increasing our own financial security, enhancing our sustainability, or trying to stay afloat can never really be the true heart and soul of stewardship. Taking a risk *for* others with the gifts we have been freely bestowed with, however, is plainly foundational to an authentic calling. It is what the incarnation is all about. The risk God takes in Jesus is that there are no returns for total love.

Yet God still loves us, even if there is no return on that commitment. God asks us to love the world in the same way. That is bound to be a risk, and there will be losses and rejections. Jesus knows that too. One might say that the best motto for stewardship comes from Lord Tennyson's poem 'In Memoriam A. H. H.', written after Tennyson's great friend Arthur Henry Hallam died very suddenly: ''Tis better to have loved and lost than never to have loved at all.'

Quite so. The investment of love was not wasted. It was better to have risked the love and lost it, rather than keep yourself to yourself. Or, as that other great architect and practitioner of expansive loving stewardship, St Francis of Assisi, put it: 'It is in giving that we receive, and in dying that we are born to eternal life.' Or, if you prefer a more modern idiom for the kingdom of God: 'It's the economy, stupid' (Jim Carville in 1992, writing for Bill Clinton). Maths rarely deceives us in the financial markets. Likewise, in the church, what we count, bank, invest, share and give away tells the world all it needs to know about where our hearts lie and where our treasure is (Matthew 6:21).

We can argue the toss (of a coin?) as to whether currency, in its broadest sense, is the same as money. They are plainly different. Currency is about more than money, and dwells on value, reciprocity and exchange. God's only currency with humanity is love. As the mystic Julian of Norwich observed: 'We are so preciously loved by God that we cannot even comprehend it.'[2] For God, humanity is precious and worth any price.

So we can only think about the specifics of money once we have thought about the deeper issues of value – how we value each other, our values, how God values us, the values we place on the world, humanity and the planet. We also need to consider who and what lacks value. All talk of money flows from this. It does not drive it.

Thus, stewardship is not about holding on to what you've got or clinging to the little you might have been given. It is, rather, about seeing that the gift is God's love, and if you don't share it, use it and risk it, there can be no returns, interest or hope for the church. The currency of the kingdom of God is love, and we are asked to risk it, share it, grow it and invest it.

Good stewardship is about working beyond the church and seeing the world as God sees it. That is what the kingdom of God is. Good stewardship can only be directed to that end. Ultimately, God's kingdom is a cashless economy where the only currency is love.

So, ask what God would have you freely give to others, and then go on and invest in that work. Just as Jesus and the early church did too. Trust me, it will be worth the risk. Whether you succeed or fail, you honestly can't lose.

Part 1
Mission, ministry, money

1

Two sides of the same coin

Then the Pharisees went and plotted how to entangle him in his words. And they sent their disciples to him, along with the Herodians, saying, 'Teacher, we know that you are true and teach the way of God truthfully, and you do not care about anyone's opinion, for you are not swayed by appearances. Tell us, then, what you think. Is it lawful to pay taxes to Caesar, or not?' But Jesus, aware of their malice, said, 'Why put me to the test, you hypocrites? Show me the coin for the tax.' And they brought him a denarius. And Jesus said to them, 'Whose likeness and inscription is this?' They said, 'Caesar's.' Then he said to them, 'Therefore render to Caesar the things that are Caesar's, and to God the things that are God's.' When they heard it, they marveled. And they left him and went away..

MATTHEW 22:15–22

This gospel story is sometimes accompanied by a subheading: 'Render unto Caesar'. The essential underlying core of the exchange appears to be Jesus explaining to his critics that you give to God what is due to God and do likewise with the civic authorities. Simple enough, I guess. Except the question put to Jesus is a baited trap, as the Roman Emperor is a god too. So, in a way, one is potentially both colluding with idolatry and financially supporting an occupying power.

To state that this gospel story is taxing would be something of a pun. But taxing it is, and perhaps the most important thing to note from the outset is that this exchange between Jesus, the Pharisees and the Herodians is one of the most misunderstood passages in the gospels, and that has been so for every century since the original incident. But why?

Even before we dive into this, how can this story be framed as 'two sides of the same coin'? The phrase refers to two different but closely related features of one idea, such as two ways of looking at the same situation. Thus, according to some people, great opportunity and great danger are two sides of the same coin. Equally, rewards and punishments are two sides of the same coin since, in some respects, both are used to control people. As life teaches us, neither reward nor punishment works very well. This story from the gospel says the same. Sometimes, neither option is entirely right.

Some have used this passage to justify the civil and legal orbit of government power, and it reminds Jesus' followers to be good citizens wherever they reside. I don't dissent from that interpretation. But the passage is about money and taxes, not about obedience. So, I wonder if it might help us to ask some questions of the past in order to understand our obligations as citizens and Christians in the present – from whatever country you belong to.

Taxes. When did you last hear a sermon on taxation? Or a good explanation of taxes from the church that made you think taxation might be quite a rewarding subject, and not just a topic to grumble about? (No, me neither.) But if we start with taxation, we can begin to think ourselves into this exchange and incident with the Pharisees and the Herodians. So let me make some observations about systems of ancient taxation.

First, Joseph and Mary were taxpayers. The census at Bethlehem recorded in the gospel of Luke is a 'head count', but also the basis for leveraging a tax on citizens. Joseph returns to the place of his birth to be registered. That registration would have resulted in some kind of annual tax falling on each household.

Second, in the Roman Empire, there were four primary streams of tax revenue: on cattle, land, customs (imports and exports) and the profits from any profession, which would include Joseph's trade as a carpenter and builder. There was no income tax. The taxes were there for the same reasons they are now: funding security, the military, public works, transport networks, upkeep of roads and stimulating the economy – they all need support. Zacchaeus, Matthew and others are named as tax collectors in the gospels. Raising taxes was vital for social flourishing then, as it is now.

Third, the ancient Roman Empire also divided their taxation into two streams. One stream of tax – known as tributes – was levied on land ownership, which was effectively a wealth tax. The other mainstream of taxation was the poll tax, which covered inheritance, auctions (including slaves), sales and even postage. City states could also levy local taxes and the Roman Empire also permitted licences for religious taxes.

This brings us, neatly enough, to the gospel of Matthew. And here, it always pays to ask: where does this encounter take place, who was present, what was at stake and why does it matter? Here, having done some maths, we need to do some geography. And the first question is, where is Jesus *from*?

The answer is, though born in Bethlehem, where Joseph registered for the poll tax, Jesus is in fact an ethnic Galilean and Nazarene. This matters, because Galilee was not part of the Roman Empire. At the time, Galilee was a kind of 'client province' of the Empire – under the heel of Rome, but allowed to be ruled by the Herodian dynasty.

Herod and his son, Herod Antipas, were the client 'kings' in the lifetime of Jesus. They were effectively puppet rulers – tetrarchs – there to keep order on the edge of the Empire and granted titles and freedoms in return for loyalty and obedience.

This is important, because when it comes to the trials of Jesus prior to his crucifixion, Pilate washes his hands of the affair because Jesus, as a Galilean, is not subject to Roman law or jurisdiction. Nor is Jesus subject to Judean law. Yet Jesus is also not subject to Galilean law, as his alleged crimes are committed in Roman territory – and they are not crimes under Roman or Galilean law. The Sadducees, scribes and Pharisees want Jesus put on trial under Jewish law, but neither Herod nor Pilate can oblige. The high priests argue blasphemy should lead to the death penalty, but the only way to achieve that end was to *avoid* a trial altogether, and judge and condemn Jesus without due legal process. That is what happens. Remember Caiaphas' words: 'What further witnesses do we need?' (Matthew 26:65). Caiaphas does not think Jesus should have a legal process because, were that to happen, he'd likely be acquitted.

I raise this here because you might think Jesus is 'rendered to Caesar' in the false accusation and mockery of legal processes and trials he undergoes. But the phrase 'Render to Caesar the things that are Caesar's, and to God the things that are God's' is not only about tax and money. It is about Jesus himself, and you and I, and the wider world. Jesus will be rendered to God – to whom he belongs. Lots will be cast for Jesus' clothing, to be raffled by Caesar's soldiers. What you have belongs to the world – you cannot take it with you – but you belong to God.

Jesus, of course, is no fool. He's a consummate politician. The question he is asked is 'Is it lawful to pay taxes to Caesar?' Jesus answers with a different verb: 'Give *back* to Caesar what is Caesar's and to God what is God's' (NIV). Jesus does not deal with paying tributes. In other words, the quizzers have answered their own question. The Herodians and Pharisees used and benefitted from Caesar's economy so that their tribute was not a gift but simply what was involved in that economy. That fits with Solomon's 'For all things come from you, and of your own have we given you' (1 Chronicles 29:14).

The question-and-answer session recorded in Matthew 22 takes place in Jerusalem, so lots of monetary currencies would have been legitimate. But what of the coin in this encounter? Note that it is Jesus who asks to see a coin. The coin was not one preselected by his trickster-accusers, and it must have surprised his questioners that Jesus demanded to see the currency. A *denarius* is produced. But what else could it have been?

There are seven coins named in the New Testament (see Appendix II to find out more). The value of coins lay in their weight as well as their size. Old English versions often translate the coinage as 'pennies' and 'farthings'.

But the real history is more interesting. The lightest was the *lepton*, usually known as the 'widow's mite' (see Mark 12:42; Luke 12:59; 21:2), and had the least value.

The *drachma*, in contrast, was a silver coin that was heavy enough to be a bridal dowry, and would be passed from mother to daughter. The coin could not be spent commercially, but would have family, senti-mental and actual value. It is this coin that is referred to in the parable of the lost coin. It is an extremely precious coin, akin to something like losing your mother's wedding ring.

The *didrachma* was a smaller silver coin, and it was exchanged in the temple, and equal in value to a Jewish shekel. But Jews were not permitted to use their own silver for coins under the treaty terms with Rome. The *didrachma* was minted in the city of Tyre – a Gentile city – and the coin bore the head of Baal. So, moneychangers in the temple were needed because a good Jew could not make an offering or temple payment using a coin that bore the image of an idol and false God.

The *didrachma* therefore had a specifically religious purpose as legal tender. You might be able to use it for ordinary day-to-day purchases, but as coins, they were also essential for taking inside the temple and exchanging for shekels so as to offer any kind of offering, object or service.

Now, you might think that dedicated religious currency used only for religious purposes is part of ancient history – that such brazen financial shenanigans and leveraging of obligations all hails from a very long time ago and that no modern faith would impose such religious taxes on its people. But you'd be wrong.

Think, for example, of the practice of 'Peter's Pence', in which every home was encouraged (and later obliged) to contribute 'one penny-per-hearth' (i.e. fireplace – sometimes called 'smoke money') to supplement the costs of the See of Rome. That practice began in England in Saxon times and continued through the Reformation. Even after that, some parishes in England continued to pay the See of Rome 'Peter's Pence' well into the 17th century, presumably 'backing both horses', so to speak, despite the Reformation. Some manor houses belonging to Roman Catholic families continued paying the tax until the late 19th century.

In 1871, Pope Pius IX formalised the tax across Christendom, with an annual collection taken on the Feast Day of St Peter and St Paul (29 June). Today, the custom of Peter's Pence survives, with the money sent directly to the Holy See in the Vatican, to be used for philanthropic purposes. Current estimates of this annual global collection suggest it may amount to more than $100 million each year. However, this tax is not without its critics, since it was revealed in 2019 that the income had been invested in luxury properties and speculative ventures such as the movie *Rocketman* (a biopic of Elton John) to make more money.

In medieval times, there was also the sale of indulgences, in which Christians across Europe were encouraged to contribute to the buildings and maintenance of the Vatican. The indulgences courted controversy for their *quid pro quo* ethos, namely that as part of the prayers, good works and sacramental obligations of good (Catholic) Christians, financial giving would also benefit those souls in purgatory, longing to be in heaven. Purgatory – from the word 'purge' – is a doctrine of the Catholic Church that argues that only fully cleansed souls can enter heaven. Purgatory was therefore a kind of 'spiritual washroom' in which souls were prepared for lasting eternity. The prayers, sacrifices and good works of those still living could, it was thought, reduce the time a loved one – a soul – stayed in purgatory.

With the Protestant Reformation erupting in 1517, the sale of indulgences became a central issue, as they were characterised as 'spiritual credits' that could supposedly be cashed-in to reduce time in purgatory. The practice was lampooned by critics. Figures such as Johann Tetzel, a German Dominican Friar (1465–1519), were singled out for particular criticism. Tetzel was effectively 'head of sales and marketing' for indulgences across Christendom. It was Tetzel who coined the phrase (no pun intended): 'When a coin in coffer rings, a soul from purgatory springs.' (Perhaps not the catchiest example of a strapline in an advertising campaign, but it did at least rhyme.) Martin Luther challenged the sale of indulgences and thereby questioned the reality of purgatory itself. For Luther, the very idea that money could expedite a soul's release from purgatory was anathema. Luther regarded such teachings as unbiblical, undermining core doctrines such as salvation by faith and Christ's grace alone.

In more recent times, there have been notorious examples of financial abuse, including the 'health, wealth and prosperity movement' and other faith-healers convincing people to make significant offerings of money to support the ministry and lifestyle of the preacher. Then again, there are good examples of honest exponents of tithing, with churches strongly encouraging their congregants to give ten percent of their pre-tax income to the church and charitable causes.

The Herodian dynasty had its own coinage too; a kind of Royal Mint in Jerusalem which produced the silver shekels that Jews could trade in. But there were few in circulation. Most people used *quadrantes, assarii* and *denarii* – which were like US dollars today – everybody had them. That was the currency of the Roman Empire, and it is one of those coins (the *denarius*) that Jesus holds in his hand, and asks whose image is to be seen.

Even here, there is some religious ambiguity. Is the image of Caesar that of a pagan ruler, false god or foreign idol? The Pharisees could have argued so. Is the image of Caesar that of a tyrant heading up an illegal occupation of Judea? Herodians might argue that.

The entrapment that Jesus is contending with is therefore very sophisticated. Will he endorse Baal – the old, false god we find in the Old Testament? Will he endorse the new gods of Rome, or Caesar as a legitimate dictator? Is Jesus going to suggest a third way, which incites economic and political rebellion? In fact, his answer avoids all these bear-traps: you give back to God what belongs to God, and you give back to the authorities what belongs to the authorities.

Tellingly, in the gospel story that follows this passage, Jesus is questioned on who a wife belongs with at the resurrection if she has been married to each of the seven brothers in her earthly life. You might think this is a story about marital fidelity. But it isn't. This is about possession and ownership. The wife belongs to nobody in the end. Jesus does not regard the woman as a chattel to be inherited, possessed or divided up. She is, first and foremost, a woman. Matthew records, with characteristic understatement, that 'when the Pharisees heard that [Jesus] had silenced the Sadducees, they gathered together' (22:34) – gathered together, we know, to plot to kill Jesus.

Jesus, by evading the money-trap, also throws the question back to us. How are we meant to live? Jesus' answer – or at least the one clear principle you can infer from the story – is that his followers are obliged to follow the law, but also to *exceed* the law.

The only laws Jesus ever actually resisted were punitive religious codes. It is often assumed that Jesus' ministry embraced all-encompassing forgiveness and indiscriminate compassion. Yet we note the gospels record no such sentiments directed by Jesus towards the religious leaders of his time, who presided over a culture that systemically oppressed and abused others.

This collective group – scribes, Pharisees, Sadducees and chief priests – were seen as agents of injustice, protecting their power and prestige. When the moneychangers are whipped in the temple by Jesus, you can see something of the anger he harbours for religious hypocrisy and exploitation. It is a planned attack by Jesus too. He sees the corruption in the morning and assaults later in the afternoon, after he has made a whip to drive out the moneychangers (see John 2:13–22).

Arguing with Jesus must have been hard work 2,000 years ago. Not that I think it is any easier now. Jesus was alive to the social, political and economic ambivalence of his time. Herod's alliance with Rome brought Judea money, employment, trade and stability. It came at a price, however. The Roman symbol of the golden eagle had been erected directly outside the temple and, as a symbol of foreign might and idolatry, would have been difficult for religious hard-liners to stomach.

Herod's taxes would not have been popular, but were any taxes ever popular? While on the one hand Herod used taxation for civic enterprise, on the other, his expensive tastes for luxury imported goods and lavish entertaining were well-known and deeply resented.

Ultimately, the message to us is this: our true citizenship lies within God's kingdom. We belong to God. But we still give to earthly powers what is their due.

We have obligations as citizens to support others in our service to society. The services supported include the work of our education systems, social welfare, good government, law, order, police, emergency services and security. Even the Roman Empire provided roads, water, policing and sometimes relief for the poor. We may not always agree on the type or extent of services our governments should provide, but we are obliged to contribute to society to help those who cannot help themselves.

Finally, let me say a few words about the Pharisees. They get a bad press in the gospels, for sure. But the reasons why they were resented (if indeed they were) have been filtered through two millennia of church tradition. Most Christians assume that the Pharisees serve as some kind of cypher for nitpicking attitudes to the law of Moses that gave them power and even a financial uplift. Tithing dill and cumin, after all, seems almost pointless and would appear to be religiously burdensome to the point of being oppressive.

However, such views are wide of the mark and hail from centuries of antisemitism. Pharisees were, in fact, rather expert at getting around the law of Moses, and are better thought of as consultants specialising in tax-avoidance schemes. That does not detract from Jesus' critique of them. Indeed, his remarks make more sense. But it does help explain why the Pharisees, while plainly loathed by many, were nonetheless loved by the wealthy few.

So, render to Caesar what is Caesar's. Render more to Caesar if you can, exceed in your civic duty, and excel at being a good model citizen. Jesus protested against punitive religious laws but did not take issue with secular authorities.

And render to God what God requires of you. And if you can, exceed that too, as God's own must. Go the extra mile. Give all you can. Remember the words of Brother Roger of Taizé: 'God will never ask too much of you… but he will demand everything.'

2

Money magic

> When they came to Capernaum, the collectors of the two-drachma tax went up to Peter and said, 'Does your teacher not pay the tax?' He said, 'Yes.' And when he came into the house, Jesus spoke to him first, saying, 'What do you think, Simon? From whom do kings of the earth take toll or tax? From their sons or from others?' And when he said, 'From others,' Jesus said to him, 'Then the sons are free. However, not to give offense to them, go to the sea and cast a hook and take the first fish that comes up, and when you open its mouth you will find a shekel. Take that and give it to them for me and for yourself.'
> MATTHEW 17:24–27

This has to be one of the showiest miracles recorded in the gospels. Moreover, it is entirely concerned with customs and revenues, which, as we shall see, are managed in a manner bordering on satire. While in Galilee, Simon Peter gets into a conversation with two temple tax collectors who want to know whether Jesus pays his dues. The phrasing of the question suggests that the tax collectors think Jesus does not. The situation is seemingly resolved by an innocent live fish being turned into a temporary ATM – a pescatarian cash machine. So, is this a miracle that really shows off some pretty astounding magic? Or is it, rather, something else? It is the latter, of course.

Over the centuries, the funding of the Church of England has also utilised echoes of the 'temple tax', the most obvious example being tithing. This was a ten percent tax imposed on the yields from land, farming and product output in any parish. In addition, the church also owned land – called glebe – the yields and profits from which went directly to support the parish priest. Other methods of funding clergy and ministry came through patronage (e.g. from the wealthy lord of the manor), endowment and private chaplaincy. This system of funding the church existed from Saxon times and continued uninterrupted beyond the Reformation, finally dying out in the mid-20th century.

Tithing from rural parishes produced controversial and occasionally comical anomalies. Prior to the Industrial Revolution, parish clergy were usually the local enforcers of the tithe-tax that paid their living costs and provided revenue for the upkeep of the church buildings, and additional ministry costs such as relief for the poor or the provision of schooling. But ten percent of yield is an imprecise framework for taxation. It led to ructions and occasional riots.

For example, in the 18th century some farmers complained that clergy, in claiming ten percent of the income derived from a given field, were asking for a tenth of the proceeds from the straw, milk, butter and cheese that one field might produce. In protest, the clergy might find a considerable amount of milk, butter and cheese dumped unceremoniously on their altar at the dead of night – still given to God, yet unsellable now, as large amounts of dairy produce tipped all over the altar were not easy to do anything with. In the 19th century, some Cornish clergy tried to claim ten percent of the proceeds from what the local fishermen were landing. The fishermen went on strike, arguing that parish boundaries did not extend into the North Atlantic. The clergy countered that the quayside was in their parish, and anything landed there to be sold merited a ten percent levy. Quantities of fish were duly dumped on altars in protest. In the 20th century, Kentish farmers were rioting about tithes as late as 1935.

Clergy could resort to extreme measures in collecting tithes and dues, and their widows could follow suit too. Since 1718 the Revd John Gamage had been rector of Sedgefield, County Durham. He wasn't there much, on account of his also being a canon of Salisbury and a vicar in Worcestershire. But he travelled north every year in December to collect his tithes.

He had form, as they say. Between 1739 and 1741 he'd been locked in a legal dispute with local landowners refusing to pay him tithes. He sued, they countersued, and the case was settled eventually in the High Court, with costs awarded against the landowners. When the Revd Gamage did venture north, he resided in Sedgefield's huge rectory, which was about the same size as the parish church of St Edmund, almost next door.

However, the Revd Gamage died in Worcestershire in August 1747, meaning that his widow, Mary, would be unable to collect the tithes from the recalcitrant villagers of Sedgefield. Undeterred, she pickled her husband's body in a barrel of brandy (or possibly using salt instead to preserve it), transported him north in December, dressed him and arranged that his corpse be seated at his desk, clearly visible in the front parlour to all passers-by. She then removed his body after a fortnight or so – only after enough villagers had noted he was residing in Sedgefield – but explaining that he'd had to return to Worcester on urgent business. She duly went around the village and farms collecting the tithes on his behalf.

The deceit took decades to unravel, and when it did, the villagers retaliated with arson. They waited until the rectory was vacated, as it frequently was, and set it ablaze. Today, and perhaps inevitably, this extraordinary story (be it folklore or true) has led to the village gastropub being called 'The Pickled Parson'.

You might imagine that the haphazard 18th-century tithing system, patronage, endowment and private support for ministry tended to produce generations of priests mired to either perpetual penury or great wealth. Certainly, the system produced stark inequalities. Charles Darwin (1809–82), writer of *On the Origin of Species* (1859), rejected his father's counsel regarding employment. Robert Darwin wanted his son to be a rector of a parish or to follow in his footsteps and be a doctor. While Charles studied medicine at the University of Edinburgh, he chose to pursue his passion for the natural sciences and in 1831 boarded *HMS Beagle* to voyage as the ship's naturalist. The rest, as they say, is history.

If Charles had become a parish rector, what kind of income could he have drawn from an 'average' rural parish in a year? One biographer suggests £300, which would equate to around £30,000 today. Darwin, or probably his father, would have bought the 'living' (as parishes were known) at special auctions in London where parishes – depending on the income they generated – could be procured for several thousand pounds. So, a smart investment.

Bear in mind that Darwin would not have needed to be ordained to be the rector of a parish, nor could he have trained for ministry, as there were no seminaries and divinity (or theology) was only offered as a graduate degree at Oxford, Cambridge and Trinity College, Dublin. Incidentally, in the 19th century, medicine was a one-year graduate course, while theology was a three-year slog, which says a lot about hierarchies of knowledge back in the day.

So, if you wanted to own a 'living' but avoid the labour of three years' of theology, one way forward for drawing an income in the 19th century was to become a lay rector. If you were wealthy enough, you could buy several of these wherever they happened to crop up for sale. An ordained curate cost somewhere between £50–100 a year to hire and could be installed by the rector. The reside of the tithe income, cottage rents and other dues went to the incumbent who possessed the 'living'. The rector was under no obligation to be ordained or to reside in the parish, let alone the vicarage or rectory, and need not necessarily provide housing for the curate either. You do the maths, as they say.

As Adrian Desmond and John Moore noted in their biography, Charles Darwin's father was a confirmed freethinker and:

> Sensible and shrewd. He had only to look around him, recall the vicarages he had visited, and ponder the country parsons he entertained at home. One did not have to be a believer to see that an aimless son with a penchant for field sports would fit in nicely. Was the Church not a haven for dullards and dawdlers, the last resort of spendthrifts? What calling but the highest for those whose sense of calling was nil? And in what other profession were the risks of failure so low and the rewards so high? The Anglican Church, fat, complacent, and corrupt, lived luxuriously on its tithes and endowments, as it had for a century. Desirable parishes were routinely auctioned off to the highest bidder. A fine rural 'living' with a commodious rectory, a few acres to rent or farm, and perhaps a tithe barn to hold the local levy worth hundreds of pounds a year could easily be bought as an investment by a gentleman.[3]

The systems for collecting (apparent) dues from hard-pressed parishes have evolved over time. As tithing rapidly collapsed in the wake of the Industrial Revolution, the Church of England was, for some while, able to leverage support costs through the rates charged to districts and parishes by local government. This too, had its problems. Only Church of England buildings and work qualified for support from the rates, which jarred with those already funding their own denomination, or who were not religious at all. Furthermore, if there was no Church of England building in your district, then no rate could be levied. This explains the occasional instances of city-dwellers engaging in arson on newly built 19th-century churches.

The latter part of the 20th century saw tithes vanish, clergy stipends regularised and new modes of securing finances to prop up the buildings and ministry of the Church of England. Such schemes are usually quite opaque on what it is, exactly, that those contributing are paying for. Often dubbed 'parish shares' or 'ministry and central costs' and the like, it is now essentially a matter of individuals in congregations reluctantly being herded into some 'paid-up members' scheme. With rare exceptions, the ministry received equates to the ministry that the congregation can afford.

And so we come to the temple tax collection in Galilee. The temple is not in Galilee, but in Judah. Galilee in the time of Jesus was overseen by Herod Antipas, and it was effectively a client state of the Roman Empire. Judah was occupied by Rome, in contrast, and governed by Pontius Pilate. So, the very presence of temple tax collectors in Galilee is something of a puzzle. Just imagine the Archbishop of Canterbury despatching hirelings or 'stewardship advisors' to collect 'dues' off English-born Anglicans living in parts of the UK outside England, or in the wider world, to support the refurbishment and upkeep of Lambeth Palace or Canterbury Cathedral. (I think we all know how that might land.)

The gospel writers concur that Capernaum was Jesus' second home. On the northwestern shore of the Sea of Galilee, it was a trading point with a fishing industry. The population during the time of Jesus was around 1,500 people, so classed as a town (or even city). It was garrisoned by the Romans, had a customs house, one (or maybe even two) synagogues and would have been multilingual and multicultural. Just as Bethlehem means 'the town of bread' (and where Jesus, the bread of life, was born), Capernaum literally means 'the place of a disorderly accumulation of objects'. So here is Jesus, dwelling among the mess and disorderliness of first-century Palestine. It is not even clear who is ultimately running Capernaum, never mind Galilee.

We can perhaps presume that the temple tax collectors are on a speculative mission, trying to collect dues from Galileans to send back to Judah. And perhaps Matthew is suggesting that the very question put to Simon Peter is leading: 'Does your teacher not pay the tax?' Peter says Jesus does. But it is not a Roman tax or a civic tax. It is, rather, a religious tax – the half-shekel equivalent of what every adult male over the age of 20 was required to pay in Mosaic law towards the upkeep of the tabernacle (Exodus 30:11–16). Peter's answer to the tax collectors is hurried, presumably because he is anxious to ensure Jesus is regarded as a good Jew and not in any way disloyal or dishonourable to the faith – that Jesus keeps the law of Moses.

But when Peter returns to the house at Capernaum where Jesus is, Jesus immediately asks him about this taxation: 'From whom do kings of the earth take toll or tax? From their sons or from others?' There is only one right answer here: 'From others.' To which Jesus replies, 'Then the sons are free' (or some versions of the Bible say 'exempt'). Tax-exempt? Yes, but there is more going on in this brief exchange than immediately meets the eye.

This story comes after Simon Peter has affirmed Jesus as the Christ, for which Simon is named 'Peter' and declared the rock upon which the church is to be built. In that context, Jesus' speech on taxes and customs are part of the reset that is now taking place. Jesus has told his disciples that Christ 'must go to Jerusalem and suffer many things from the elders and chief priests and scribes, and be killed, and on the third day be raised'. Peter refutes this, to which Jesus replies with a swift rebuke: 'Get behind me, Satan!' (Matthew 16:13–23).

Jesus only ever calls Peter 'Simon' on the occasions when he lapses back into his old ways of thinking. It is a chastisement and encountered in the gospels where Peter is trying to prevent Jesus from fulfilling his calling through suffering and death (e.g. Luke 22:31 – 'Simon, Simon, behold, Satan demanded to have you'). So, Jesus' call for a fiscal reset falls within the same vein, with the disciples being instructed to rethink their lives through the lens of kingdom values.

The two *didrachma* tax is equivalent to the Jewish half-shekel, and unlike duties on goods or taxes and tributes paid to the Roman Empire, this tax falls on individuals. But when it comes to the coin extracted from the mouth of the fish, it is a *stater* or shekel. In other words, the miracle is that Jesus' 'magic moment' is paying for both himself and Peter. But this is not a matter of prestidigitation (i.e. a conjuring trick performed by sleight of hand for entertainment). The miracle is not some kind of 'magic money trick'.

The coin found in the mouth of the fish means something else. Jesus is signalling: that the children of the kingdom of God are exempt and free in relation to the tabernacle, temple and access to God; that God's grace, love, mercy and presence are free; that Jesus stands with and shares this freedom with Peter as a free son too; that a relationship with God is no longer a taxing burden, obligation or cost to us. Jesus has provided here, quite literally, the means of paying for free access to God. And, at the same time, managed to slightly belittle the tax in the process.

Was Jesus a payer of this tax from the age of 20? Probably. But now his ministry has begun in earnest, every gesture of compliance and resistance has political and moral meaning. The Tyrian shekel was the most likely coin to be conjured from the mouth of the fish. It is the same coin that Judas receives 30 of for his betrayal of Jesus. The Tyrian shekel, sometimes known as *tetradrachma*, were legal Jewish tender, but minted by the Romans in Tyre.

On one side of the coin they bore the image of the pagan god Baal (and later Beelzebub), wearing leaves from the Tyrian games. On the other side of the coin was an eagle, symbolising the power of the Roman Empire. Although Matthew does not specify what fish carried the *tetradrachma*, it is traditionally thought to be the freshwater tilapia.

There is another sense in which two sides of the same coin are here in these verses: danger, yet opportunity; pain, yet reward; suffering, yet salvation. This is a coin toss (or coin-flip). Does Jesus pay the temple tax? How do you call it? Heads or tails? Peter calls it wrong. In calling Peter 'Simon' once again, Jesus issues a gentle rebuke, sharply reminding Peter that he must inhabit a renewed mind, and not revert to his old ways of thinking.

But I digress. The miracle is that, whether Simon Peter calls heads or tails, gets it right or wrong, Jesus provides the coin. Even if you call it wrong, you can't lose. Christ has paid. Regarding this miracle being two sides of the same coin, we have the central and core issue over free and restricted access to God and God's free and unrestricted love for us. The currency of the kingdom of God that Jesus proclaims and practices will no longer be about taxes, dues, obligatory customs, precision in gestures, or acceptable cleanliness levels policed by scribes, Pharisees, elders and teachers of the law.

The purpose of the miracle is to make a point about freedom and exemption from oppressive taxes and obligations imposed by some domineering, self-serving religion. This is why in the gospels, Jesus says the temple will, in any case, be destroyed. It has become a customs house, a place of financial exchange.

Yet Jesus claims that what will replace the destroyed temple will take only three days to make. What is coming now will be a new kind of temple, made of flesh, one full of love, kindness and abundant mercy. It will come with free access to all, regardless of status, personhood, ethnicity, ability or capacity. It is nothing less than the body of Christ – a temple of the Holy Spirit, in other words, that is free for all.

3

Rewards and bonuses

When evening came, the owner of the vineyard said to his fore-man, 'Call the labourers and pay them their wages, beginning with the last, up to the first.' And when those hired about the eleventh hour came, each of them received a denarius. Now when those hired first came, they thought they would receive more, but each of them also received a denarius. And on receiving it they grumbled at the master of the house, saying, 'These last worked only one hour, and you have made them equal to us who have borne the burden of the day and the scorching heat.' But he replied to one of them, 'Friend, I am doing you no wrong. Did you not agree with me for a denarius? Take what belongs to you and go. I choose to give to this last worker as I give to you. Am I not allowed to do what I choose with what belongs to me? Or do you begrudge my generosity?' So the last will be first, and the first last.

MATTHEW 20:8–16

Parables are subversive media for communicating truth. C.H. Dodd, the great British scholar of the New Testament, defined a parable as 'a metaphor or simile drawn from nature or everyday life, arresting the hearer by its vividness or strangeness, and leaving the mind in sufficient doubt about its precise application to tease it into active thought'.[4]

For Jesus, the everyday perception of the world was false, decep-tive and misleading. For most other people, this was the only world that existed. The parables of Jesus mark the frontier of a new reality. They mediate that reality by helping those on this side of the frontier cross over to the world beyond. That beyond is an alternative reality, a strangely familiar but frightening new country. Those who glimpse that far country are both charmed and repulsed. They are simultaneously attracted and repelled.

The parable of the labourers in the vineyard explores fairness, income support, benefits, wages and collective responsibility in a challenging economic situation. At the most basic level, the grapes will spoil if the harvest is not collected in the allotted time. If that were to happen, income and profit for the vineyard would be depressed. Consequences flow from that: lower wages for all next harvests, fewer jobs and more poverty.

The parable, therefore, pivots on the need to get the job done quickly, which means using labour that might otherwise not be engaged under normal circumstances. Indeed, the workers hired towards the end of the day are the dregs. Those who are last to be hired are, de facto, the least employable.

Clearly, the vineyard is a workplace. In Palestine, as with other agrarian economies, the window for harvest is short, and the grape harvest comes just after a season of heavy rain. So, the vineyard owner needs the maximum number of workers for the minimum time. The workers themselves are day labourers – the most insecure, powerless and exploited of all. They are hired by the day and paid at sunset. They have zero-hour contracts. So, an idle day is a hungry day, for the wages described in the parable are only enough for a family to live on for one day.

The parable introduces some surprises even before we get to the end. As the sun sets, the labourers line up for their pay. And this is where the trouble really begins. For a start, the (perhaps weaker) men who were hired last are paid first, and to their great surprise they get a full day's wage. Those who have been at work all day (likely the stronger) rub their hands in anticipation – obviously, they will get a day's work and a bonus! But, of course, they don't; it's the same wage for everyone, irrespective of how hard they have worked. No wonder the cry comes, 'That's not fair!' Well, that's the story. But what does it mean in terms of currency and economics?

In the 1992 US presidential election, a senior political consultant to the Democratic party, James Carville, came up with three quips for Bill Clinton to use in televised addresses. They were 'Change versus more of the same', 'Don't forget healthcare' and 'It's the economy, stupid'. It is the last of these that has been entered into the textbook manual of political campaigning. Clinton was up against George H.W. Bush, whose approval ratings were very high. The three quips are substantially credited with changing minds in America, leading to Clinton beating Bush.

In one sense, churches are as concerned with their ecology and economy as any other body. The term 'ecology' derives from the same Greek word for 'church', *oikos*, meaning 'household', 'home', or 'place to live'. Oikology (or *oekologie*) concerns the relation of the person to both their organic and their inorganic environments. Ecology is conventionally regarded as a scientific term and discipline. However, it is also used in the humanities and social sciences and can encompass religious geographies, social patterns and outlooks (e.g. class, race, wealth, etc.) and the relationship between groups and their environment, as well as other groups.

One of the first ecologists was Thomas Malthus (1766–1834), the English economist and demographer. He put forward his theory that population growth will always outstrip food supply. He worried that there would not be enough to go round. If so, who pays more, who gets less and how does a government, denomination or church survive when there is not enough to sustain everything?

The Church of England has yet to adapt to the economy in which it finds itself; namely, one in which a comprehensive national ministry is now funded by congregations rather than its parishes. True, as a 'spiritual public service' to the nation, the Church of England continues to enjoy a modest (though declining) degree of public support at many levels. It still seeks to continue serving all of its people. But all its people do not fund the church. In fact, only a few of the people have done so haphazardly throughout its history.

In bygone eras, the tithing of the whole community supported the local parish church – both the building and the clerical stipend. Up until the 16th century, non-payment of tithes could mean excommunication, while non-attendance could merit a fine. But fines were always difficult to collect and seldom imposed, and excommunications were almost unheard of. The practice of tithing was always haphazard, and it waned quickly in direct proportion to the growth of industrialisation throughout the 18th and 19th centuries.

Parliamentary reforms in 1836 tried to regularise tithing by replacing the notoriously chaotic ten percent levy imposed on all produce with further rental charges imposed on land. But even this could not last, and in 1868 the law abolished the church rate (which had been re-imposed in 1661). As late as 1935 there was a demonstration against tithes in Kent, at which an effigy of the Archbishop of Canterbury was burnt. The practice of paying a tithe on land wasn't finally abolished until the Tithe Act of 1936.

What the church rate had tried to achieve was to put national religious provision on a more stable footing, as it obliged parishioners to financially support their parish church (irrespective of their beliefs and commitments). But the cultural and industrial revolutions of the 17th and 18th centuries questioned this arrangement intensely. Parliament passed the Toleration Act in 1689, enshrining religious freedom in law. The freedom to worship where you wished inevitably inferred permission to support your own religion in your own way – and to not subsidise the established church. By the last quarter of the 19th century, the foundations for the present anomaly were already laid; namely, the bifurcation of the economy of the parish with that of the welfare of the parish church.

However, parish churches were to be open and available to their respective resident populations and were to minister to them accordingly. The cost of that ministry, however, was borne not by the parish but by the congregations themselves and in collaboration with the Ecclesiastical Commissioners. By the 20th century, further reforms to the financing of the Church of England had placed more power in central and diocesan hands. In 1976, the Endowments and Glebe Measure vested all land and its management in the hands of its host diocese.

Measures were taken throughout the Victorian era to try to close the gap between excessive wealth and poverty that the clerical stipends delivered. Even in the 19th century, there were wide variations in clergy pay. The Archbishop of Canterbury was paid £19,000 a year, equivalent to around £2.7 million today. In contrast, some curates might only receive £50 a year, equivalent to about £7,000. In fairness to the archbishop, his income came from 300 parishes that he was notionally rector of, so he had the responsibility of staffing those churches and their upkeep and would have had to do the same for Lambeth Palace, his home in Canterbury and other lodgings scattered around other parts of the country. There were other oddities too. The twelve canons of Durham cathedral received £3,000 a year each and the dean of Durham was also the bishop of St David's, Wales.

Close attention to the history of monetary support for ministry allows us to make three distinct observations within the context of the parable of the labourers in the vineyard. First, and perhaps obviously, wealth creates the basis for independence. In both the pre-Reformation and Hanoverian age, when religious orders or parish clergy were economically prosperous, 'religious professionals' enjoyed power and status, and were free to define their role within society. The first batch of workers in the parable are agile, mobile and more independent than those hired at the end of the day.

Second, when the wealth of church began to disappear in the 19th and 20th centuries, clergy were inevitably pressed into deeper collusive alliances with their congregations and dioceses, who were quickly becoming responsible for providing their funding. This led, inevitably, to a gradual loss of independence for parochial clergy, creating a culture of dependency.

Third, as John Dolan notes, the relationship between clergy, congregations and money has affected all denominations, including those that sought to minister within a working-class culture:

> The people are groaning under the pecuniary burdens which are imposed upon them from time to time. One collection follows another in rapid succession, and they never know where the misery will end. There are more than seventy collections every year, either public or private – was this always the case? We answer, it was not; a time was, when Methodist preachers had little more than fifty pounds per annum; their wants then were few, they laboured for souls, and success in their labours was to them a sufficient recompense. Superfine coats, water-proof hats, silk stockings and gold watches were never the object of their pursuits. Surely, Sir, this cannot be said for the present race of Methodist Preachers.[5]

The parable of the labourers in the vineyard is instructive here. 'That's not *fair!*' is a cry that nearly every parent dreads yet knows only too well. Children develop a keen sense of justice early on, especially when their own desserts are at stake! Our society – with its industrial disputes, waiting lists and public anger over fat cats and inflated bonuses – is conscious of fairness. Surely, reward should be distributed according to merit, and pay should be related to work done? It would appear in this parable that the complainants have a very strong case, and most members of any church congregation would agree with them. But as with nearly all of Jesus' parables, there is more to the story than meets the eye.

One way of interpreting the parable is to focus on the equality of pay. In other words, the vineyard owner is acting mercifully by making sure that all have enough money to feed and clothe their family. John Ruskin, more than a century ago, wrote four articles in the *Cornhill Magazine* that were eventually published as a book with the title *Unto This Last* – which is a quotation from this particular text. Ruskin's exposition of the parable was an eloquent attack on the economic theory of his day. Ruskin was an associate of F.D. Maurice and Charles Kingsley (author of *The Water Babies*), so Ruskin's exposition has a close association with early Christian socialism – New Labour before there was even Old Labour. Ruskin, in his exhortation, pleads for a sort of minimum wage, describing the parable as offering a pattern for the Christian care of the underprivileged and the powerless.

Whatever you think of that interpretation, it certainly has some merit. But there are deeper meanings in the parable that lie even beyond this social and political exposition. In this respect, it is useful to distinguish between what is fair and what is generous, and the relation between earnings and needs. The parable makes a delightful play on our own childish conceptions of fairness in relation to the vineyard, which I take to be a cipher for the kingdom of God. Here's my point. The generosity and the justice of God are so abundant that it is, in the end, deeply *unfair*. The parable is aimed at the sort of people whose sense of virtue or fairness makes it difficult for them to allow God to be generous to those who have done less well.

In other words, here's a parable that questions our motivations and our reasoning. Do we really feel that we have 'earned' God's favour? If we work, we earn our wages. But earning God's love is not possible, as it is unconditional and free. This is what the economics of this parable drives at. If everyone gets the same wages, then surely the real, true, keen, loyal and hardest-working hirelings must get bonuses? I mean, it is surely only fair that their loyalty and hard work, not to mention their superior productivity and greater sacrifice, is worth *more*?

The parable refutes that. For your highly productive disciplined dis- cipleship, and faithful following throughout your life, irrespective of adversities and sacrifice, the parable speaks. It says you will have your reward. The sting in the tale, however, is that those who may have done far less will receive the same as you do. The wage, bonus and rewards scheme is, in other words, flat. The currency of the kingdom of God assumes equity. Christ died for all. God loves all. Favouritism and hierarchy have no place in this economy of God. (Granted, the parable of the talents repudiates the lazy worker or fearful investor, but that story is making a different point about faith, and not trying to imply that some kind of inequality in salvation can be presumed.)

So, we have a parable that seems to side with the lazy, the publicans and sinners, or those who've done less well or worked less hard. Or those who perhaps cannot work, through no fault of their own, or were just never chosen or even asked. The currency of the kingdom of God is very fluid, and it seems to be available in equal measure to everyone. There are no extra rations for harder work. There is no loyalty clubcard and bonus points in the rewards scheme for those who have shown exclusive devotion to one master.

This is, in other words, a terrible parable for the church. But that's salvation for you, isn't it? In the war between Jesus and the church, the church is ahead on points, but it is a war it cannot win. God will open his kingdom to whom he chooses; all are invited. You are not the gatekeeper. You are not God's immigration officer or border security. The kingdom of God does not have a problem with desperate migrants or illegal immigrants. Citizenship is given to anyone who asks.

The gospels offer extreme cases of this. The dying thief on the cross is an obvious example. He could not have worked in the vineyard for more than a few seconds, let alone an hour, yet on the cross, for the most minimal confession, he is promised paradise. A few words, and Jesus replies with no hesitation: 'Truly, I say to you, today you will be with me in Paradise' (Luke 23:43).

Had the disciples still been around to witness this exchange shortly before the death of Jesus, they must have wondered to themselves what on earth the point of giving up everything and forsaking all for the kingdom of God had been. Had they not been with Jesus for three years? Had they not abandoned their jobs? Had they not left behind their families, even leaving the dead unburied? Of course they had. So how come, then, Jesus is offering precisely the same – no more and no less – to a man who has been committed to a lifetime of violence and crime? Precisely. It isn't fair, is it?

The parable gets right under the skin of the real motivation for being part of the church and following Jesus. And the interesting thing that the parable suggests is that in Christ's scheme of salvation, the rewards and bonuses scheme is rather flat. In other words, salvation does not come in half measures – you cannot be half saved; you're either welcomed into God's kingdom or you're not. You cannot be half ordained. Salvation doesn't come in fractions. You cannot be half baptised. You either receive the Eucharist or you don't – sacraments are not divisible.

And so the parable, as many do, comes back to haunt the church. Instead of policing the borders and the boundaries of God's kingdom, we are invited instead to gather up everybody – as many as we can – to share in precisely the same fortune that we already enjoy and perhaps have known for years.

This takes us to the parable of the prodigal son and asks whether you're enjoying the feast, celebrating with the younger son who was dead but has been miraculously brought back to life. That's what the party is for. Or, whether you're bitter and resentful with the older brother, believing that the party and celebration is undeserved and ill-afforded. The economics outlined in the parable points to the foolish abundance, the ridiculous generosity of God in relation to whom he bestows his favour on. Mercy and grace are infinite, and all shall receive the same. As budgets go, it is good news for those who start each day with nothing.

It is the same salvation for the bishop of 25 years, the priest of 50, the reader of 75, or the church warden who has put in 100 years of hard graft, blood, sweat and tears into keeping their church going. Or the sides-person who remembers the foundations of the church being laid way back in 705 by the Saxon Bishop of Eealdhelm – 'I was there then, and I'll be here after you've gone, young man.' It is the same salvation for the tiniest child who is baptised right at the end, or indeed for those in the middle, who stumble around in their half-belief, perhaps even barely caring about the inheritance that has been bestowed upon them. James Carville was right: it's the economy, stupid. This is kingdom economics. The last shall be first, and the first shall be last.

In all of that, the parable of the labourers in the vineyard asks, do we, as the church, rejoice at God's abundance or seek to limit, privatise and control it? This parable amplifies God's resounding 'yes' to those who have nothing. And in turn, this parable questions the accessibility and openness of churches and their ministries. We can't be in the business of turning anyone away, because God's emphatic loving 'yes' – his invitation to all – is still on offer. As F.W. Faber's inclusive hymn puts it:

There's a wideness in God's mercy
like the wideness of the sea;
there's a kindness in his justice
which is more than liberty.

There is no place where earth's sorrows
are more felt than up in heaven;
there is no place where earth's failings
have such kindly judgement given.

For the love of God is broader
than the measure of our mind;
and the heart of the Eternal
is most wonderfully kind.

But we make his love too narrow
by false limits of our own;
and we magnify his strictness
with a zeal he will not own.

There is plentiful redemption
in the blood that has been shed;
there is joy for all the members
in the sorrows of the Head.

There is grace enough for thousands
of new worlds as great as this;
there is room for fresh creations
in that home of upper bliss.

If our love were but more simple,
we should take him at his word;
and our lives would be all gladness
in the joy of Christ our Lord.[7]

4

Economic miracles

> On the third day there was a wedding at Cana in Galilee, and the mother of Jesus was there. Jesus also was invited to the wedding with his disciples. When the wine ran out, the mother of Jesus said to him, 'They have no wine.' And Jesus said to her, 'Woman, what does this have to do with me? My hour has not yet come.' His mother said to the servants, 'Do whatever he tells you.'
>
> Now there were six stone water jars there for the Jewish rites of purification, each holding twenty or thirty gallons. Jesus said to the servants, 'Fill the jars with water.' And they filled them up to the brim. And he said to them, 'Now draw some out and take it to the master of the feast.' So they took it. When the master of the feast tasted the water now become wine, and did not know where it came from (though the servants who had drawn the water knew), the master of the feast called the bridegroom and said to him, 'Everyone serves the good wine first, and when people have drunk freely, then the poor wine. But you have kept the good wine until now.' This, the first of his signs, Jesus did at Cana in Galilee, and manifested his glory. And his disciples believed in him.
>
> JOHN 2:1–11

The miracle of the wedding at Cana in Galilee is a story rich in analogy and symbolism. But it is also packed with a telling litany of detail that should make us reflect more on our place within God's world. Most people remember the story for the result – an absurd amount of very good wine produced at the end of a feast in which, presumably, many have already had quite enough and won't be riding their donkey's home.

But consider this. For the miracle at the wedding to happen at all, two people have to take the risk of falling in love and declaring that they want to spend the rest of their lives together. Several people had to draw and fetch large amounts of water to make wine. To make the huge jars which held the water, and later the miraculous wine, someone had to dig the clay, stoke the oven, mould the clay and fire it. And someone had the final headache of organising a Jewish wedding and hundreds of guests. Without these 'base', ordinary materials, there is no miracle at Cana. We all have our part to play in the transformations and miracles that are wrought by God.

The gospels remind us that basic and perhaps rather unpromising materials can be transformed when offered to God. Ordinary bread becomes the body of Christ; ordinary wine his blood. And yet it is essential to remember that these materials remain as they are, even as they are transformed. In a church that is sometimes obsessed with being pure and holy, we need to remember that every version of Christianity has a local accent. Every type and form of Christianity is incarnated within its local culture – time, space and life.

The story of our faith is, in other words, a story of common, local water turned into wine – the transformation of what is base, drawing out the very best of what that life or material is, to a new and redeemed status. Put another way, it is the blessing of reality. Our faith is just that.

This is why Paul's well-known phrase is right: '[His] power is made perfect in [my] weakness' (2 Corinthians 12:9). We do not belong to a religion where power finds expression in perfectionism. Instead, we look for the God who is incarnate, who comes to the world and is found in human form. God *uses* our weaknesses – the foolish and base things of the world – to work his changes. But whereas we look for perfection, God looks for the weakness – he is drawn to it, because he seeks to not only change it, but to actually work through it.

As the mystics say, if God has a weakness, it is his heart – too soft. There would have been people at the wedding in Cana, therefore, who would have been sipping the wine, but perhaps not agreeing with the steward's expert verdict that the groom had saved the best until last. You can perhaps imagine dissenters muttering: 'Well, he says its good, but personally I don't care for these new fruity Mediterranean wines myself. I've never liked Pinot Noir grapes. Give me a good claret any day, made from the Merlot grape variety.'

But that's the thing with God: it is indiscriminate love. Ten lepers are healed; only one says, 'Thank you', but the other nine are nonetheless stilled healed. At Cana, everyone was served wine and drank; only a tiny few knew the inside story.

The miracle at Cana in Galilee also belongs to a broader context, namely one of perpetual hunger, the constant risk of harvests failing and therefore famine and death. The very appearance of excess and bounty in the stories that Jesus told, the miracles he performed and the encounters others had with him are atypical of most people's day-to-day experiences. The gospels are set in a time when food is scarce, yet the super-rich can build storehouses for grain and hoard. Food riots, rocketing inflation and the possibility of starvation are never far from people's experience. As Luzia Sutter Rehmann has argued so compellingly in her *Rage in the Belly*, famine, fury and the shape of society are powerfully interconnected in today's world, and more so in the time of Jesus.[7]

The dynamics of hunger, starvation, famine, plenty, greed, harvest, drought and social unrest over food shaped the world that Jesus knew. We in the northern hemisphere lack a 'hermeneutic of hunger' with which to read the gospels. As we do not know hunger ourselves, we forget how much of Jesus' life revolved around his hunger and thirst, and that of others, especially the poor.

This is perhaps why the earlier appearances of John the Baptist are so important in this context. His critiques of the political and social status quo are also economic challenges. They are also challenges and withering critiques of the scale of religious collusion with unjust economic and social policy. We see this critique acted out early on in his ministry.

John the Baptist ate locusts (Matthew 3:4, which the KJV tells us was 'his meat'), almost certainly out of sheer desperation. Locusts are usually only plentiful in times of famine. But we perhaps forget that following Leviticus 11:20–23, there are only eight types of locusts that are kosher. The Talmud also informs us, helpfully, that there are over 800 non-kosher species of grasshoppers and locusts. So, for every hundred, only one can be eaten. As locusts swarm, it is pretty likely that despite the clouds of them, though nutritious, they will be prohibited protein sources. So, in mentioning that 'locusts were his meat', we are introduced to a perpetually hungry man in an age of food short- ages, regular famines and economic austerity. We are being offered a comment on a faith that insists on being picky even when faced with overwhelming hunger for its populace.

It is against this background that the miracle at Cana in Galilee belongs, with its absurd quantities of wine and the potential for limitless, if not excessive, feasting and celebration. But lest there be any doubt about the politics of excessive and abundant food, consider the parallel stories of the miraculous feeding of the 4,000 and the 5,000.

The ministry of Jesus is startling in its inclusivity. It is customary, in a kind of lazy-liberal and somewhat reductive way, to suppose that the gospel writers simply got their maths muddled and were a bit confused about a single event. But in fact, there may be good reasons to regard the two miracles as quite separate. The feeding of the 5,000 takes place on the western banks of the Sea of Galilee. The region was almost entirely Jewish, and the twelve baskets of leftovers symbolise the twelve tribes of Israel.

What, then, of the feeding of the 4,000, and the seven baskets of leftovers? The event occurs on the eastern shores of the Sea of Galilee, and the region was almost entirely Gentile in composition. The seven baskets of leftovers correspond to the seven Gentile regions of the time (i.e. Phoenicia, Samaria, Perea, Decapolis, Gaulanitis, Idumea and Philistia). Moreover, the baskets (*kophinos*) in the feeding of the 5,000 are smaller than those mentioned in the feeding of the 4,000 (*spuridi* – a basket big enough for a person, as with Paul in Acts 9:25). The point here is that the new manna from heaven will be distributed evenly, across all lands. There is plenty for all. The gospel of Christ is, in other words, radically inclusive: Jew, Greek, Gentile, slave, free – all shall be welcome in the kingdom of God.

But to return to the miracle at Cana in Galilee, there is also something else worth paying attention to. It is to ask who gets the blame if the catering arrangements fail and the bar runs dry? Here, I think we are asked to take note of Mary, the mother of Jesus, who perhaps perceives that the stewards and workers (or even slaves) serving the food and wine will be punished for their catering failure and wine-lapse.

This story shows how both Jesus and Mary are attentive to those with little power who yet carry the ultimate responsibility. If the wedding feast fails, the shame falls on the families hosting. In turn, their shame would have to be atoned for, and while that might mean some financial compensation, it would almost certainly result in retributive acts taken against those serving the food and wine. The consequences for them would be punitive and grave.

The miracle at Cana overcomes shame and loss and is a reminder of God's outrageous and surprising abundance. A wedding that runs out of wine would be humiliating then, as it would be now. The miracle speaks to us: God's love and grace are not measured out – in ration-book tokens, as it were, with a finite supply. Grace and love are infinite. It is there for all in ridiculous, stupefying and intoxicating quantities. His love flows and flows and flows. This miracle speaks of his extravagant love and generosity. It says that even at a wedding reception, God lavishes his love on those whose gaze is wholly elsewhere.

But there is something else that connects these miracle stories of abundance of wine, loaves and fish, and they point to a much deeper economic miracle. Gavin Francis is a GP, and his book *Intensive Care* reflects on the nature of pandemics and how we respond. What I admired most about the book was his neat summing up of the skill that a GP needs for the role: 'science with kindness'.[8]

Not enough is written about kindness, yet it is an essential core element in most vocations, and arguably most professions. It is also essential for economics and stewardship. Actually, kindness is one of the major core currencies of humanity. I used to remark to students at Cuddesdon that once they were ordained, most mistakes and faults would be forgivable. Bad preaching is not ideal, but it is tolerable. Poor administration is not helpful, but it is unlikely to be the deal-breaker between parson and parish. That then raised the question: 'What is the deal-breaker?' I would counsel ordinands that they must be two things (good and kind), at least, and these were non-negotiable. They had to be *good* and *kind*. Good, in the sense of virtue – honest and decent. And kind in that everyone would know that this priest, come what may, would be gentle, humble, loving, patient and of service. Good people, full of goodness and ideally overflowing with the milk of human kindness. This meant that in being good, they must also be utterly dependable.

Kind and good. That is what we need from our clergy, and it is not a bad thing in our GPs and others who work in caring professions and vocations. These are also the watchwords for our politicians and economies. As for the church, I'll take a good pastor any day, over and against an untruthful and bad person, even if they are a brilliant preacher, liturgist, administrator or leader. Goodness, kindness and truth matter most. Yes, most of all. Being kind and good matters.

For the earliest churches, goodness and kindness spilt over into sharing the good news. That good news was not a mere sermon, however. Good news meant actions, lifestyle, kindness and sharing. There was no good news for the poor if it just turned out to be a newsflash from a street preacher ranting about sin and salvation. Good news for the poor meant a good church, and truthfully, *feeding* the poor, and keeping them warm and in shelter, treating them with dignity and kindness.

The goodness and kindness at the heart of Christian faith is Jesus, the living bread. The shared meals and feeding of those who could not feed themselves extended from the very heart of the Eucharist. Just as Jesus, the living bread, is for all, so was the church to be a community that fed and nurtured the widows, orphans and those who could no longer care for themselves, or whom society (or religion) had discarded.

Bethlehem, where Jesus was born, means 'House of Bread' in Aramaic and Hebrew. So, from the crib, to the last supper, to Emmaus, and to our altars today, the bread we share is *banal* – common food, symbolic of spiritual and inward nourishment, that binds us together as one equal body.

Common food and common eating are the hallmark of equality in fellowship. When training for ordination, my wife Emma and I spent a year on placement in Consett in County Durham. The economic ravages of Thatcherism had decimated this once proud steel town, and rates of unemployment were high, along with the other accompanying indices of health, obesity, smoking and long-term depression. Yet working with the curate and community was a source of endless, utter joy. The congregation and parish were terrific company and moving exemplars of resilience and hope.

It is the leaven of the communal suppers and lunches that Emma and I often recall, over 30 years on. For the menu was always the same: corned-beef pie, sometimes served with a side of boiled potatoes. We never quite got the hang of the recipe, but it was essentially corned-beef mashed with potato and filling an 'envelope' of short-crust pastry. It is fair to say that as a meal, it was filling. Indeed, I sometimes wondered, with the winds whipping off the moors, if the function of this food was partly as ballast. The top layer of pastry was not latticed, and it came as it came, hot or cold.

The appreciation for this local Consett fare lay in its commonality. We all ate of one social meal, and it bound us together, so there was no enmity or competition in the provision of food, cooking skills and class, taste or other particularities that might divide us. Corned-beef pie meant something: this is us – we share our social life, lot and fellowship together.

There is one body. One pie. Irrespective of education or occupation, or the lack of either or both, there was no room for any sneering snobbery when it came to food. All partook of one meal.

Years later, when Emma became vicar of a parish in Sheffield, the congregation's typical meal was meat, potato pie and minted mushy peas. Again, you might think, more ballast than nutrition. Perhaps. But this standard, repeated menu had a quasi-Eucharistic function. This is how we expressed our life together socially, not just liturgically. Like bread and wine, the typical meal for social occasions expressed our unity and our equality. Goodness and truth meant that we ate together as one, because we were committed to the goodness of unity.

So, pie was for sharing. In Switzerland, most hamlets still remember and celebrate the community bread-oven located in the centre of the village, with the loaves apportioned out as each person and household needs through the long winters. This work was regulated in each community by a 'banal' – our word for 'common', but the Swiss term for the village council that looked after everyone, so fostering the common good.

In the same vein, I think of the powerful testimonies recorded in Abby Day's study of older Anglican women, who form the backbone of the pastoral care in churches by baking.[9] Day notes how the women gather in the kitchen of the church hall and bake hot-cross buns, which are then distributed around the parish to those in need. Economically, this makes no sense in strictly monetary terms. It is plainly far, far cheaper to go to any supermarket and buy the buns in packs, probably in some 'three-for-two' deal. But homemade buns to somebody grieving, recovering from an operation or recently divorced and finding it hard to step out of their house say something deeper: 'We care, and you matter.'

Day also observes how the act of baking itself, collectively, binds the women together in caring, kindness and kinship. They look out for each other, and each of the women involved in baking has a task that is inherently assigned value. Some make the dough. Others source the ingredients. Others prepare the small parcels to be distributed later. Like the miracle of the loaves and fishes or the wine at Cana, we rarely think of the value ascribed to those tasked with distribution, and how much it might mean to them. The economy of God is not just materials or money. It rests on kindness and equality of value.

So just how does God make the ordinary into something that begins to speak of transformation, overflow, grace, extravagant excess and lavish love? Simple: bring yourself and what you are and offer it. And remember that marriages, like weddings, need work and support. As the unknown author of the poem 'A Good Wedding Cake' has it, once you've mixed in the ingredients of love, laughter, wit, forgiveness, common sense and more besides, you complete the recipe by working the whole together and baking gently. And, adds the poet, you do this for a long time, because marriages never reach that point of perfection. They are never complete.

Marriage is often about attending to simple things. You can tot up lots of things in a marriage. Years. Rows. Holidays. Mistakes. Celebrations. Pets come and go. Children too. But at the risk of stating one thing here that I hope is obvious, marriages are basically ordinary things that can be made special – and even extraordinary. But to be so, they need to have feet firmly planted on the ground.

One writer I often quote is the sociologist Peter Berger. In one of his books, he reminds us that marriages are essentially open, extended, evolving conversations. So, we must learn to listen and tune in; yet also learn to speak. To know when to say something and when to be silent, and to learn from what we give and receive.

Marriages are somewhat like people: basically good, but never perfect. Conversations are like that too. So, if you want to see a bit of a miracle, you can actually help to make one. But it is by attending to the small details that the miracle is made. Make a pot; fetch some water; arrange a wedding; commit; do all the ordinary things you usually do.

But do these things with open eyes, hands and hearts. And ask God to transform the small and ordinary. Offer yourself, and ask God to use your ordinariness, and perhaps even your weakness. Ask God to use a wedding, a union, a friendship, a partnership or a marriage. And just as God pours out his Spirit, so will you be poured out, in surprising and abundant ways.

5

Crumbs of comfort

> Jesus answered, 'It is not right to take the children's bread and throw it to the dogs.' She said, 'Yes, Lord, yet even the dogs eat the crumbs that fall from their masters' table.' Then Jesus answered her, 'O woman, great is your faith! Be it done for you as you desire.' And her daughter was healed instantly.
> MATTHEW 15:26–28

There is nothing better than a welcome surprise. A welcome surprise can energise, replenish and reassert the course of your life. Whether a kind gesture from a stranger, an unexpected call from an old friend during a tough time, a new and surprising connection, or a much-needed and unprompted embrace, such moments remind us that we live by both faith and the element of surprise.

Gerard Hughes, a Roman Catholic writer, explores the centrality of surprise in faith in his book *God of Surprises*. You may be on a path of complete assuredness, far from God – perhaps a committed atheist, a long-term agnostic or a believer who has taken their faith for granted or lost a deep sense of it: the God of surprises catches all off guard.

I used to ask my theological students: 'Do you think Jesus got a surprise at the resurrection?' Some said no, of course not; others surely covertly dismissed it as a silly question. I'm not sure that anyone concluded that he might have. My own response was more than mischievous. I said Jesus lived by faith and died in faith, and when he was raised from the dead, it is likely he got the most tremendous surprise, such is the life of faith.

The well-known Christian apologist C.S. Lewis mirrored this in his book *The Lion, the Witch and the Wardrobe*. The children discover that Aslan the lion returns from the dead, having been killed by the witch. They ask him why, if he knew that this was to be, he didn't spare them the grief and sadness of his death. Aslan, as the figure of the risen Christ, simply says that although the hope of such a thing had been longed for since ancient days, it hadn't happened before and so who could tell?

If living by faith is to live with the possibility of being surprised, the question follows: could anything have surprised Jesus? If this question fills you with doubt, then remember: Jesus is forever travelling and always seeking new connections, and he crosses into a new region of Tyre and Sidon (Matthew 15:21). It's a geographical boundary, but full of new prospects, the possibility of meeting people on the fringes of Israel, and therefore those considered outsiders.

The gospels are full of encounters between boundaries of race and religion; for example, the story of the Samaritan woman in John's gospel or the account of the Gerasene demoniac in Matthew, Mark and Luke. But in Matthew's gospel, we have already met the Roman centurion – certainly one of them, not one of us. This time it's someone else. 'And behold, a Canaanite woman from that region came out' (Matthew 15:22).

As Jesus moves between boundaries, he is met by someone who is also moving to seek him out – that's the sense of the text, of reciprocal movement. The Canaanites were the original inhabitants of Palestine, treated with scorn and as traditional enemies of Israel. I imagine Jesus being trepidatious at the prospect of the encounter. The woman (not named, just known as a Canaanite) started shouting, 'Have mercy on me, O Lord, Son of David; my daughter is severely oppressed by a demon' (v. 23). This marks the first time in Matthew's gospel that a woman addresses Jesus, and she happens to be an outsider. She calls him 'Lord' and 'Son of David' – unusual, as most encounters include one but not both identifiers. And as the encounter continues, this woman shows she is full of surprises.

We might say she has an extremely high Christology, more Jewish than the Jewish. Jesus does not answer her at all. He ignores her profound appeal for her daughter, who is suffering from some form of epilepsy. Even today, this affliction devastates people's lives and those of their families and friends. It is met with silence from Christ. Perhaps he doesn't want to know. Or perhaps it gives him pause to take a moment to prepare a response. Several commentators have suggested that the woman is left dangling as if Jesus is waiting for his moment.

But there is no doubt that his lack of response surprises the hearer of this gospel. To see Christ so dismissive in the face of such need and distress is wounding to those of faith. In our lives, rejection from those we hold in the highest esteem, or perhaps with the greatest authority, is deeply hurtful. In the story, Jesus' disciples urge him to dismiss the woman outright, to stop her following them and to cease her desperate pleas for help. We are not left in doubt of their response – they are explicit. No silence from them. One response is to give the woman what she wants, to 'get rid' of her – after all, she is Gentile.

Jesus finally breaks his silence. He shares the harshness and prejudice of his disciples: 'I was sent only to the lost sheep of the house of Israel' (v. 24). In this moment, he is a pious Jewish teacher, the role emphasised by Matthew's gospel, which seeks to root Jesus in his religion and people. Our understanding of the crucial relationship between Christianity and Judaism has been greatly enhanced by discovering the Jewish Jesus. The embrace of this identity at times makes for some hard edges. It's an 'us versus them' world. I'm for us and not for them.

Today, influential people seem to know precisely who they are and where they are. The 'us versus them' world is the toxic centre of our culture and politics. In anxious and uneasy times, when conflicts dominate our news, the temptation is to simplify things into the binary. The 'us versus them' world is the foundation of fundamentalism in all its guises, whether religious or political or built into attitudes to the economy, class, gender, race or nation. It is alluring. After all, in embracing this world view, you know where you stand; you know who you stand with and who you are against.

There is comfort in such assurance, but it is alarming. Looking across the expanse of history, we see that such easy divisions are how dictators, authoritarian rulers and those monopolising power prefer to order the world. Furthermore, these figures want people to see the world in this way. It is clear and easy. It also ensures violence, conflict, stereotyping and scapegoating. It creates a world without grace, without generosity and nuance. It is a world without surprise.

The story of the Canaanite woman is striking for many reasons, and it sits within a fascinating chapter in Matthew's gospel. Matthew 15 begins with Jesus and the disciples being taken to task for not complying with strict ritualistic hygiene laws. Jesus responds, ending with a caustic and offensive criticism of this religious world view. Jesus rounds on his critics and says we are not defiled by what comes into our bodies, but rather the stuff that comes out of them.

The miracle story of the Canaanite woman's daughter might almost be a parabolic illustration at this point. In terms of ritualistic protocols, Jesus should give her a wide berth. But the woman's plight now marks the transition from tribal religious compliance to a global gospel. The woman has needs and is desperate. She also has faith and is persistent. The woman reaches out across boundaries as a Gentile to a Jewish rabbi and healer, begging even for just some crumbs of comfort. She is rewarded with the bread of life. Ask, and you shall receive. Seek and you will find.

After this encounter, as though to emphasise the change of focus in Jesus' mission, the feeding of the 4,000 takes place. This is like the feeding of the 5,000, which took place on Jewish territory. The feeding of the 4,000, with different numbers to symbolise it is a separate event, is for a hungry Gentile audience. The message could hardly be clearer. Kingdom catering serves everyone now, not just 'the lost sheep of the house of Israel'.

There is no doubt that Jesus' response to the Canaanite woman is hard to process. Many a commentator has tried to understand the episode in softer ways – Jesus is merely testing her; he really has something up his sleeve, just wait. But this smoothing over obscures the offensiveness of his silence. What is remarkable and surprising is that this woman does not give up. She is othered, despised and discriminated against again. But her purpose is strong: 'She came and knelt before him, saying, "Lord, help me"' (v. 25). She humbles herself, placing herself and her daughter at his mercy. If we could rewrite this story as we want, we might say Jesus reached out to her, lovingly took her hand and prayed for her daughter, ending the story in joy. As recorded, Jesus answers, 'It is not right to take the children's bread and throw it to the dogs' (v. 26).

This is a harsh statement, depicting the Jewish privilege of that time. Dogs are scavengers, predatory working animals treated as pariahs – far from the household pets we cherish today. The dog was an inferior creature and a standard Jewish image for Gentiles. The woman replies, 'Yes, Lord, yet even the dogs eat the crumbs that fall from their masters' table' (v. 27). That is quite a response – to say, in effect, 'Yes, that's all true, I am a Gentile dog, but...' Matthew's gospel positions the people of Israel as children of the table. This woman refers to the 'master's table', and the dogs are under the table; they are in the house. Three times, she refers to Jesus as *Kurios*, Lord; now it is the master's or the Lord's table. As a Gentile, she claims a fringe benefit of the blessings of the God of Israel.

I think this response comes as a surprise to Jesus. Does it change his mind? Scholars debate this. In my mind, it is more than a simple change of mind. Being taken wholly by surprise by this woman's humility and faith, Jesus has a heart, mind, body and soul conversion. He might say, I wasn't expecting that from a Gentile dog. He responds: 'O woman, great is your faith! Be it done for you as you desire' (v. 28).

Jesus has the realisation that someone he initially considered as worthy of contempt, an 'other', a foreigner, one of them, not one of us, is, in fact, more pious and fuller of faith than anyone could ever expect. It is not simply a matter of 'your faith' but 'great' faith. It's the faith of one in the tradition of the psalms of Israel who cries out, 'Lord, have mercy.'

There are further resonances to address in this story, not least the crumbs that come from the bread. Are crumbs really enough? The sense of society being divinely ordered lies behind such initiatives. Although it remains a much-loved hymn, few people today sing the third verse to 'All things bright and beautiful', written by Cecil Frances Alexander in 1848 as part of her collection *Hymns for Little Children*:

> *The rich man in his castle,*
> *The poor man at his gate,*
> *God made them, high or lowly,*
> *And ordered their estate.*

The hymn reflects similar theological notions of divine providence ordering the hierarchy of society and sustaining it as part creation. Alexander was, interestingly, Anglo-Irish, and it is likely to reflect her view of the Irish peasantry that she would have known as a wealthy landowner. Her view of social strata both sacralises and affirms the existing social order in the midst of the Irish Famine, the worst year of which was 1847. Percy Dearmer, the Christian socialist and hymn-writer, expunged the third verse from his *English Hymnal* (1906). He took exception to the implicit inertia and passivity the verse expressed in the face of such devastating social inequality, and openly opined that the hymn reflected the world view of a wealthy woman brought up as the daughter of a land-agent on an Irish estate.

The apparent lack of Alexander's cognisance of the story of Dives and Lazarus (Luke 16:19–31) also struck Dearmer as rather odd. The parable of Dives and Lazarus is a judgement on our indolence. Are you too preoccupied to notice, too busy to help? There is judgement for that.

Then there is the other kind of bread. It is the one we are given manna-like, without ever asking. The Feast of the Annunciation – the visit of the angel Gabriel to Mary to tell her the 'good news' that she was pregnant and would bear a son – falls on 25 March, exactly nine months before Christmas. The immaculate timing of the annunciation is a proclamation of the immaculate conception of Jesus and a nine-month gestation. Since medieval times and indeed before, the Feast of Annunciation was called Lady Day. The Old (or Middle) English meaning of 'lady' was 'the kneader of bread' (*hlafdige*), and 'lord' (of the manor or a shire) (*hlafweard*) meant 'the keeper of bread'.

Even today, vestiges of the Old English meaning survive: 'dough' is still slang for money, and we still speak of households having 'bread-winners'. More colloquially, to be pregnant is to have a 'bun in the oven'. Indeed, the English word 'bun' comes from an old Gaulish and Germanic word meaning swelling or rising. Buns gestate: just watch the dough rise.

For Christians, Jesus is the bread of the world. In the gospels, Jesus takes bread and shares it: in the feeding of the 4,000, the 5,000, at the last supper and in the resurrection appearances in the supper at Emmaus and on the shore of Lake Galilee. In the New Testament, we are taught to be one body, for we all share in one bread. We are taught not to divide the body or be partial about who we feed and nourish: Jesus is for all, and his bread, as his body, is for all.

Mary the mother of Jesus is the kneader of the dough. It is her 'yes' to God and her gestation that brings forth this utterly unique fruit of the Spirit, namely the Christ-child. The crib in Bethlehem is little more than a large breadbasket. An altar at which the Eucharist is celebrated is a servery – a place from which to give that which was already freely given. As we have received this bread freely, this Jesus whom we neither earn nor deserve, so too this bread is for all who come to the supper at the table with that same Jesus who blessed and multiplied the loaves to feed so many thousands, Jews and Gentiles alike.

Mary is therefore both the 'kneader of bread' (*hlafdige*) and a 'lord' or 'lady' as the 'keeper of bread' (*hlafweard*). But she keeps it not for herself. She only keeps it to see this single dough rise and become bread for the world. She only keeps, nourishes and cherishes the infant Jesus in order to give him up. He is not hers; he is ours. And because she shares her bread from herself – flesh of her flesh – she is one with us too: the kneader, keeper and giver of bread.

Readers interested in reflecting further on this theme would be fed and nourished by John Hadley's *Bread of the World: Christ and the Eucharist today* (DLT, 1989). The sacramental theology that underwrites the book will definitely not suit all tastes. And to my mind, the writings of Richard Holloway and Gerard Hughes SJ are more grounded, though I find Hadley's notion of the Eucharist as 'heaven in ordinary' to be compelling. Jesus is an expression of God's heart for humanity. He is the body language of God. The 'kin–dom' of God is for all.

So the ministry of Jesus will integrate from the outset. It belongs in the alleys, not just the temple. It will welcome Sidonians, not just Sadducees; Phoenicians, not just Pharisees. Jesus responds to the Canaanite woman, while in John's gospel he reaches out to a Samaritan woman. He tells stories about good Samaritans, much to the annoyance of his potentially loyal Judean audience. He embraces the widow, the lame, the ostracised, the deprived and despised, and the neglected. He befriends the sinners and sinned against. He takes his tea with tax collectors. Jesus heals nobodies; the gospels, in nearly all cases, are not able to name the afflicted individuals. The people Jesus reaches out towards are excluded from the mainstream of society and faith.

What is significant about this, I think, is this. Jesus' kin-dom of God project was, from the outset, supra-tribal. It reached out beyond Judaism to the Gentiles. Indeed, he often praised Gentiles for their faith and scolded the apparently 'orthodox' religion of his kith and kin for its insularity and purity. Jesus saw that God was for everyone; he lived, practised and preached this.

We see this in the healing miracles that Jesus wrought – to a Canaanite girl, a Samaritan with leprosy or a Roman centurion's servant. There are crumbs, crusts and loaves for all. Jesus touches the untouchable, hears the dumb, speaks to the deaf and sees the blind. His healings are universal and highly partial, overwhelmingly directed to the marginalised and ostracised, such as those with leprosy or the demon-possessed. It is there in parables too, with Jesus constantly teaching us about the least, the last and the lesser. God can't take his loving eyes off the people and situations we most easily neglect.

In conclusion, the early Jewish Christian communities after the destruction of Jerusalem in AD70 had to figure out what their relations with Gentiles looked like. These communities often prized their Jewish inheritance even as they had received the gospel of Jesus Christ and the radical change this made to their lives. They had to participate in the new reality that Jews and Gentiles alike belong to one Lord. The previously robust and impenetrable dividing wall of enmity fell when faced with the life, death and resurrection of Jesus.

But the new reality was that the Bread of Christ was, and is, for all. None of us are worthy of the crumbs, yet all are invited to feast. This helps to explain why Luke, when he talks about Jesus 'receiving' sinners and tax collectors and eating with them, uses a much more dynamic word than we find in our English translations. Luke uses the word *prosdechomai* several times in his writings, and every time it means 'eagerly await or expect and look for'. So, there is a challenge to the church today. Not just to host or receive the poor, sinners and marginalised – how very English, to 'receive' such people! – but to excitedly anticipate and look out for those about to join us for food and keep us company. For we are entertaining angels. We are warmly and eagerly welcoming Christ himself.

Every generation faces the same challenge. How do you hold on to your valued identity yet be open to the surprises God has in store? This beautiful gospel story of an astonishing encounter between Jesus and someone who is not only a woman, but a true outsider, is revolutionary for the earliest Christian communities. They are called to live by faith and, with that, live by surprise. Surprise is embedded in the very life of God.

The life and facts of Jesus as a person are a testament to God's capacity to surprise and how he shares this flow of newness with the world. So, Jesus' mission is universal. There is no 'us' and 'them' – only one new common humanity. God and Jesus provided a happy surprise for the woman: her daughter was healed. May the God of surprises always wrong-foot us, and may we always have the grace and courage, as Jesus did, to be open to being wrong-footed. Let us also seek hearts of gratitude for the great faith of the woman in this gospel account. Let us follow her in living in stubborn, persistent, tenacious faith and hope in the Lord, from whose table we and all people are invited to dine.

6

Tax returns

> [Jesus] entered Jericho and was passing through. And there
> was a man named Zacchaeus. He was a chief tax collector and
> was rich. And he was seeking to see who Jesus was, but on
> account of the crowd he could not, because he was small of
> stature. So he ran on ahead and climbed up into a sycamore
> tree to see him, for he was about to pass that way. And when
> Jesus came to the place, he looked up and said to him, 'Zac-
> chaeus, hurry and come down, for I must stay at your house
> today.' So he hurried and came down and received him joyfully.
> And when they saw it, they all grumbled, 'He has gone in to be
> the guest of a man who is a sinner.' And Zacchaeus stood and
> said to the Lord, 'Behold, Lord, half of my goods I give to the
> poor. And if I have defrauded anyone of anything, I restore it
> fourfold.' And Jesus said to him, 'Today salvation has come to
> this house, since he also is a son of Abraham. For the Son of
> Man came to seek and to save the lost.'
> LUKE 19:1–10

I ought to begin by saying that at a little over five foot seven and small
in stature, I rather empathise with Zacchaeus. Too small and slight to
see the main event, he climbs to get a better view. He may be small,
but he's smart. He's my kind of man. Yet Luke's story is not really about
the height of a tax collector. So let me say more.

Luke 19 is full of crowds and numbers – first a crowd in Jericho, where
Jesus meets Zacchaeus. Then there is a parable about ten minas (or
talents) – a story of honest fiscal stewardship and kingly power. Then

there are the crowds at the next port of call, which marks the triumphal entry of Jesus into Jerusalem. Finally, we end up in the temple, where the issue is once again money. Throughout the chapter, Jesus is feted and celebrated by the crowds, who cut down palms from the trees and lay their clothes across the road as he rides through on his donkey.

The gospels record the event, telling us that the crowds lining the street to see the famous Galilean prophet and healer cried: 'Blessed is he who comes in the name of the Lord! Hosanna in the highest!' (Matthew 21:9). The event must have made quite an impact and would not have gone unnoticed by the authorities. And yet crowds can be fickle, can they not? The same people who cry 'Blessed is the King' on Palm Sunday need only a few days to change their verdict to 'Crucify him!'

The narrative involving Zacchaeus is therefore at the centre of this chapter. It is only here that the crowds and the money come together. And how Luke loves to tell his story. Zacchaeus is a small man. Small people, overall, get pushed to the *front* of the crowd so that they can see what is going on. But Zacchaeus, though small, is shunted to the *back*. He is not supposed to see Jesus – that is the point. Crowds can be cruel. The function and behaviour of the crowd are therefore an important key to understanding this story.

Crowds can be conservative, unpredictable and fickle. They can move from a frantic frenzy to a mood of relative quiet. They can be whipped up into a vicious mob or into an adoring assembly. Or they can turn the tables and be quite unmoved. Jesus spent a lot of time with crowds, and one senses that he knew how to work an audience. He used humour, pathos, irony and appeal in his rhetoric. He was persuasive. His stories hushed people by the hundreds; his sayings hit home, striking at both the head and the heart. In Jesus, we see wisdom, oratory, empathy, passion and calmness all combined.

There is another dimension to the crowds that Jesus knew, however, which ought to catch our attention as well. Amid great throngs, often pressing hard on him, and presumably jostling him too, Jesus was always strangely alert to other things. But alert to what, exactly? We already know that Jesus healed nobodies, the gospels in most cases not even bothering to name the afflicted individuals. We know that the people Jesus reached out towards were excluded from the mainstream of society and the mainstream of faith.

The people Jesus healed were mostly outsiders, whose stories were 'unpublished', which is the literal meaning of the word 'anecdote'. It is the small, unpublished stories that Jesus constantly turns to. The small man who cannot see, he sees; the small voice in the crowd, he hears; the untouched body in the pressing throng, he feels. The incarnate body is richly sensate to the 'unpublished'. The gospel tells us that Zacchaeus was rich but could not see Jesus because of 'his small stature'. So, he climbs a tree for a better look, and it is while Zacchaeus is in that position that Jesus calls to him (even though there must have been dozens of people who had climbed trees or buildings to get a better look). Jesus invites himself to Zacchaeus' house, and a new story unfolds. One of the dangers of prophetic inclusiveness.

As Mary Grey says, the healings of Jesus are 'characterised by a redemptive mutuality in which people come into their own'.[10] In Luke's gospel, it is no accident that the triumphal entry into Jerusalem is preceded by Jesus' encounter with Zacchaeus, a collector of taxes as the prelude to Holy Week. Palm Sunday begins with Zacchaeus and a profoundly discombobulating and probably unpopular social healing. Jesus once again crossed boundaries and warmly consorted with (alleged) sinners.

In Christian memory and tradition, Zacchaeus is consistently portrayed as either fraudulent or as a collaborator with the occupying Roman army. In fact, I cannot recall reading a Bible commentary or hearing a sermon in which this was not explicitly reaffirmed. The reaction of the crowd bears this out. They all 'grumbled' that 'he [Jesus] has gone in to be the guest of a man who is a sinner' (Luke 19:7). Zacchaeus, meanwhile, has decided that his response to Jesus' visit is to give half of his goods to the poor.

And then comes the hidden sting in the story, for Zacchaeus adds: 'And if I have defrauded anyone of anything, I restore it fourfold' (v. 8). That 'if' must be one of the most essential two-letter words in the gospels. That Zacchaeus is despised by the crowd is not in doubt, but nowhere does the gospel say he is dishonest. Zacchaeus is simply hated for what he does and what he represents.

So what does Jesus' action signify? That amid a crowd bestowing their adulation, Jesus refuses to side with their base prejudices. Zacchaeus is affirmed for who he is. He does not repent, contrary to how this story is read; he does not need to. Rather, a despised person is allowed to flourish, and is now seen as a figure of generosity – he has, after all, given away half of what he has.

Consistently, Jesus sides with the ostracised, the despised, the unclean and the (alleged) sinner. He refuses to allow Zacchaeus to be caricatured. He sides with someone unpopular, who one suspects has never been understood – and perhaps never been allowed a fair hearing. So, Jesus is no crowd-pleaser; he is, rather, their confounder. Even before the palms are ripped from the trees and the cries of 'Blessed!' heard, it is evident that Jesus is a disturber of crowds. He does not want their praise. He wants their commitment. And the crowds make him pay for his failure to deliver what they promised themselves.

The power of Jesus' gesture in this story should never be underestimated. And it opens up an avenue that preachers rarely explore, namely the smouldering anger and indignation of the crowd. Is it really wise for Jesus to take this on, and to be frank, is he not also angered by those who might be exploiting the poor?

We need to remember that when the subject of anger surfaces in Jesus' sermon on the mount (Matthew 5:21–26), the responsibility for it is reversed. Regardless of those who rage against us, we are responsible for holding up a mirror to those who are angry and standing our ground as a living hope for proper justice rather than a capitulation to instinctive vengeance. In so doing, we are asked not to become consumed and reduced by anger. The possibility of creating space for truth and justice can then emerge.

Our Bible translations do not always serve us well. In Mark 1:40–45, Jesus heals a man with leprosy, and most translations cite Christ as being 'moved with compassion' or 'pity'. However, a better rendering of the verse is 'moved by anger', that is, at the exclusions and marginalisation placed by society upon the man because of his leprosy. The man begs to be 'purified', the only means of social reintegration. Of course, compassion and anger are not mutually exclusive. Later, in Mark 3:5, Jesus looks at the Pharisees with anger, grieved by their hardness of heart. Later still, in Mark 10:14, translations of the Greek would be better rendered with Jesus 'losing his temper' or 'boiling with rage'. This time, the object of Jesus' anger is with his disciples for trying to prevent the children from coming to him to be blessed. Anger and compassion belong together, and we see this with greater clarity once we have learned to rescue anger from a British ecclesial polity over-invested in polite, middle-class manners and repression of anger.

Re-engaging with social, political and contextual conditions can pay significant dividends if we want to understand how widespread anger and resentment manifest across society. As mentioned in chapter 4, we lack a 'hermeneutic of hunger' in the developed world, so we fail to see how often the people Jesus ministered to were hungry and thirsty for food and water, righteousness and justice, and freedom and equity. Luzia Sutter Rehmann's work draws our attention to the 'rage in the belly' that drives anger and exhaustion through the gospels and beyond.[11] The anger caused by hunger and thirst is human, ordinary and universal. However, when hunger and thirst are not met, sullen silence sets in, which can quickly escalate into a collective rage.

Rehmann recalibrates our understanding of Jesus' actions in the gospels by showing how many critical incidents are linked to hunger. Jesus is famished in the temptation narratives. In Mark 11, the disturbance in the temple is effectively a food riot and links to the cursing of the barren fig tree. There is a geography of hunger at work in the gospels, which most modern readers miss entirely, because we have no sense of how hunger and thirst can drive anger, rage and fury, especially when those in authority overlook it or meet it with indifference. The geography of hunger also extends to the realms where justice and truth are not present – another kind of famine.

The gesture that Jesus performs by eating with Zacchaeus goes way beyond the scope of what is usually understood to be taking place in this encounter. And yet, gestures can reverse our assumptions of worth and value, and they can also subvert and convert our anger into something creative.

Let me illustrate this with two contemporary stories. The first is a popular story from World War II, which tells of a Romanian Christian who found himself imprisoned at Belsen and deprived of all he needed to sustain his faith: no crucifix, Bible, icons, devotional books, corporate worship or knotted prayer beads. So, he prayed in secret – that he might respond to the call of love. He found himself spending time in the camp with the sick, the starving, the diseased, the dying and the worst of all, the betrayers – all those who were shunned by others.

One day, as the camp drew close to liberation, an atheist priest, in fact, who had his faith shattered by the experience of war, came to see the Romanian and said, 'I see how you live here. Tell me about the God you worship.' And the Romanian replied: 'He is like me.' I wonder which of us could give the same reply. In wisdom, it is often the example that makes the difference, not the ideas; it is often the practice that counts, not the theory.

The second comes from South Africa and the dark days of Apartheid. Father Trevor Huddleston, an Anglican priest and member of the Community of Resurrection, was for a while vicar of Sophiatown – a rundown area of Johannesburg, but one of the few suburbs where people of colour could buy property. To appreciate this story, you need to picture Huddleston in your mind – a very tall, white Englishman, with a chiselled face and a rather gaunt expression. He was seldom seen without a cassock (which often appeared too short), and as an Anglo-Catholic, would also have sported a biretta.

Morning and evening prayers are said daily, so Huddleston would have frequently made the short walk from his community house up the hot, dusty road to the church, passing dozens of people on the way going about their business. Being a polite Englishman, he always raised his biretta to passers-by. And as someone who made no distinction based on skin colour, he raised his biretta to every adult he met.

His walk always took him past one particularly squalid house, where a black washerwoman laundered clothes each day, to make a living, in her tiny, cramped backyard. Huddleston would greet her and raise his biretta, while a young eleven-year-old boy played in the yard. The boy puzzled over this gesture as the months went by. Who was this white Englishman who raised his hat to a poor black woman? What kind of white man would show such courtesy and kindness? It is a simple gesture, and one that Huddleston, I expect, gave no thought to. But the boy did.

It awakened his curiosity. It sparked a thought: that all men might be equal, and that not all white men thought themselves superior. That his mother could be respected as any white woman might be. And that this priest was, in his tiny gesture, showing a new way. As it turns out, the name of that boy in the backyard at Sophiatown is known to us all: the boy was called Desmond. Desmond Tutu.

So, we might now understand something of the power of Jesus' gesture. Through hospitality and communion, barriers are broken down. The demonised turn out to be not so terrible after all. Indeed, they get preferential treatment from Jesus. They become his friends. The black woman and her son, the betrayers and the diseased in the camp, and the tax collector in an occupied country – Jesus is with them all. It is more than a mere gesture; it is a radical, inclusive communion.

Christians, it is often said, only regard themselves as honorary sinners: the rest of the world are the real ones. But the gospels faithfully preach against this nonsense. It is the self-righteous who have to rethink, and who Jesus' sermons and parables are really directed at. This is why Zacchaeus having tea with Jesus is such a profound moment in the gospels – the man the crowds want to see deciding to have a meal with the man the crowds love to hate.

This is where we find Jesus today – not with those we so easily love, but with those who we often so easily hate and lazily despise. It is as though Jesus says to each of us: 'See – he is not so bad after all. Behind the role and task he does that you detest, behold, is a generous and forgiven human being. I am going to eat with him and get to know him better.' He need hardly add: 'Go. Do likewise.' I am especially fond of this poem by Fr Robin Gibbons:

> *'Zacchaeus come down!' Jesus shouted*
> *above the noise and bustle of the crowd, over their heads,*
> *His voice like the sound of gentle thunder,*
> *rolling across the landscapes of rocky faith.*
> *Zacchaeus heard him, for he was not afraid,*
> *seeing the one who came among us*
> *in humility and love.*
> *Holding fast to the sycamore-fig tree,*
> *he could catch Jesus' eye and hold his gaze,*
> *for pure of heart he was, as is his name,*
> *able to stare into the eyes of God,*
> *his own faith filled with joy.*
> *'I am staying at your house', said Jesus,*
> *much as any friend says to a friend,*
> *'I'm popping in to enjoy good time together!'*
> *The question is, do we like Zacchaeus,*
> *recognize the Christ who comes,*
> *oft hidden by the crowds*
> *and sinful situations of our lives?*
> *We may have great consideration of ourselves,*

and yet also see
that we too are short of stature in so many ways!
Maybe we should climb up our sycamore-fig tree,
feel joyful and unafraid to respond to Jesus
both in gaze and open hospitality.
For this is the way salvation.[12]

To understand the nature of Jesus' standing in relation to the marginalised, neglected and poor, we sometimes have to read the gospels backwards from the resurrection and forward from the ascension. Jesus has a transformed resurrection body. Yet he also bears the scars of the crucifixion. And scars, as we know, remind us of the trauma and pain that inflicted the wound. Indeed, scars can still hurt us if pressed or prodded. I am old enough to remember when passports used to list any 'distinguishing features' under the photo. Mine was 'scar, lower lip', a reference to an injury I picked up as a very young child. My father had 'scar, right eye', apparently a boxing ring injury from his time of national service as a gym instructor.

But not all scars are physical, are they? Bereavement, chronic debt, abuse, betrayal, separation, loss, shame, becoming a refugee, the threat of violence, mental trauma and anguish – some scars are burned into our hearts, minds and souls. So Jesus, in the ascension, carries all these scars in his body – the external and the internal – to God in heaven. All our pain and scars are borne there.

However, from Pentecost the early church develops something new. A radically alternative 'muscle memory' when faced with trauma, loss, persecution, poverty and the like. Let me give you a concrete example. It is an old one. St Laurence was a deacon in Rome during the persecution by the Emperor Valerian. According to tradition, he fell under the suspicion of the prefect of Rome, who ordered him in three days to surrender all the treasure of the Christian church. The tradition tells us that after three days, Laurence led the prefect to a church, and opening the doors showed him the treasure. Laurence had gathered the poor, the lame, the widows and the orphans. Opening his hand, he said: 'Here is the treasure of the Christian.' Laurence was martyred – slowly roasted – for that act in the year 258.

The main issue of the encounter with Zacchaeus is not so much one penitent sinner (which is, in any case, debatable). It is, rather, the collection and reallocation of taxes, and how a crowd – likely to be hard-up and used to poverty – responds to how both a system and a person charged with the role of taxation is treated. But this is a scarred community, struggling with previous wounds, and the memories they leave inflicted on the social body. Taxation triggers trauma and pain, and Zacchaeus' seemingly preferential treatment feels like a blow landed on an old scar or hidden wound.

Jesus' actions are profoundly radical. They highlight a crucial truth: even amid a crowd eager to praise him, he refuses to conform to their prejudices. Instead, he sees Zacchaeus for who he truly is, rejecting stereotypes and standing with someone marginalized and often mis-understood. This powerful act showcases Jesus' deep compassion and transformative understanding.

Interlude:
The gospel according to Rembrandt, L. Frank Baum and Elton John

And he said, 'There was a man who had two sons. And the younger of them said to his father, "Father, give me the share of property that is coming to me." And he divided his property between them. Not many days later, the younger son gathered all he had and took a journey into a far country, and there he squandered his property in reckless living. And when he had spent everything, a severe famine arose in that country, and he began to be in need. So he went and hired himself out...'
LUKE 15:11–32

'Money talk' peppers the scriptures. The parable of the prodigal son asks some searching questions of us. How do Christians wait in hope to welcome, embrace and fully restore those who are regarded as dead to the church, yet whom God has never ever given up on – and keeps vigil for?

In the extraordinary book *We Need To Talk About Money* (Fourth Estate, 2021) by Otegha Uwagba, she takes us on a journey through her complicated relationship with money. Money talks. Money does the talking in movies like *Citizen Kane* or *The Wolf of Wall Street* (based on the life of Jordan Belfort). Money shouts from just about every page of F. Scott Fitzgerald's *The Great Gatsby*. Money makes the world go round. Perhaps that is why it can be quite so dizzying and disorientating for some. For some, it is always a head-turner.

One of the many reasons I find Uwagba's book so compelling is the way it delves into a myriad of societal issues. It's a journey filled with highs and lows, where we confront racism, class, privilege, elitism, vanity, beauty, compulsive spending, out-of-control consumerism, pride and shame. Money, always a narrative about personal security and home, is paradoxically shrouded in secrecy, reserve and repression, despite its omnipresence and purchasing power in our daily lives.

Over the years, the English language has developed a unique vocabulary for money, reminiscent of a medieval understanding of the four elements that shape our world: earth, air, water and fire. In a similar vein, money can be seen as 'elemental'. We speak of money in watery terms, like liquid assets, frozen assets, drowning in debt, flooding and reserves, and evaporating costs or profits. For fire, we can burn through money, consume or be consumed by it, and our economy can get overheated, leading to a fire-sale of assets. In terms of air, we speak of 'headroom' to breathe financially, inflation, deflation, the lungs of an economy or the chill winds of a recession. As for earth, we speak of banks, deposits, securities, troughs, slumps, economic mountains to climb, foundations, fixed assets, financial stability, and even securing funds in building societies. Sometimes these elements combine – an economic fog, for example, brings together water, air, cold and heat.

The younger son in the parable of the prodigal has, therefore, committed an *elemental* sin – almost a kind of reverse medieval alchemy in the climate. He's burned through the inheritance like a swarm of summer locusts devouring a field. He's lost his agency. There is a famine in the land, and the economy has tanked. He can only take a job as an indentured serf. He's drowning in debt. He's living in the dirt. He's lost his voice. Everything that he had, it seems, has been turned to ashes: home, family, stability, work, status, food, shelter – all gone. And for what?

He begins his journey home, half hoping that he can return to the household in which he was once a son. He's forsaken that sonship, but maybe, just maybe, his father's household will afford him some space to live, albeit as a servant rather than a son. What the son is saying to himself is, 'Look at how generous my father is. Even the servants eat well. Now, even the crumbs falling from my father's table would satisfy me more than the world offers.' The response from the father of the parable, as we know, is excessive beyond all reasonable expectation. Sonship is restored, and celebrations are inaugurated. Christmas has come early, all shame is cancelled and memory wiped clean.

Shame is one key to this story. It is easy for us to talk about what we feel guilty for – forgetting birthdays or anniversaries, a missed appointment or perhaps a stolen treat. But shame is different. We rarely talk about what we are ashamed of. Even with those who know and love us best, it is costly to say what shames us. We risk the disgust, censure and withdrawal of the one who loves us. Suppose my shame causes their rejection of me? So we keep it in. It festers.

The son felt not guilt but shame. For he knew he had shamed his father, publicly and among his neighbours and peers. The father was not ashamed of his son, but by losing his son to idle and profligate spending, he had been shamed. Diminished in the eyes of his older son, family and friends, the father finds that he, too, is ashamed.

I expect the older son thought he was doing his father a favour by staying on the farm. Charity, and maybe kindness? But it is awkward and, to some extent, possibly patronising. The father's gesture to the younger son is, therefore, revolutionary in character. Because he does not deal with shame solely by forgiveness. No. Rather, he deals with shame by redemptive, reckless, excessive public celebration – the only way to really smash shame and restore a person. Jesus does it with the woman caught in adultery, the woman who anoints him at the house of Simon the Pharisee and the Samaritan woman at the well in the gospel of John. In each case, shame is smashed – conquered by unqualified love and public vindication. Humiliation is addressed, redeemed and destroyed.

That's why the older brother can't cope. Because deep down, he's a Pelagian, the ancient English heresy that allegedly taught that one also had to work for heaven and could not simply rely upon receiving grace alone. You partly earn salvation or at least put some work towards it. God is running a secret loyalty bonus scheme. You join the scheme when you join the church. It entitles you to extra grace and special offers of God's love, and to feel ever so slightly smug. Spiritually, I mean. And provided you take your turn of duties – coffee rota, visiting others, sitting on the church council or mowing the churchyard – membership of the scheme is yours for the duration (not for keeps).

But there is something else in the economy of the parable we need to note. Most Bible versions refer to Luke's story as 'the parable of the prodigal son'. Now, if prodigious – from which we get prodigal – means wasteful, excessive and careless with what is ours, or has been given, or even perhaps taken – then there are two prodigals in this story: the younger son, obviously, but also the father, who is prodigal in welcome, love, affection, forgiveness and celebration.

Yet prodigiousness is rash, and the father is rash with what is not his. At the point of dividing the inheritance between the two sons, the older brother has acquired his half. The fatted calf, celebratory party, ring on the finger, and feasting are, therefore, not in the father's gift. They were not his to offer to others. It is the older son who is being made to pay. He wasn't asked.

There is something quite compelling in the parable about what we do when God, or perhaps the church, is prodigious with our lives and takes liberties with what is ours. We all have thresholds here, and some things we can be very relaxed about people helping themselves to without asking. But if we feel the person being helped is undeserving, we can find that we experience resentment and anger at others being generous with what is rightfully our own. And this can be even more the case if they lavish it on people who offend us, whom we are ashamed of, or who have been the cause of pain and shame to us in our backyard – well, the prodigal son and the prodigal father tick these boxes.

We can easily read the father's behaviour in this parable as a mirror of our own – worry and anxiety giving way to relief. I think this is a mistake. If we are to read this parable as the gospel writer meant it to be read, then we need to remember that he and his readers thought about family and parenting differently from how we do. Parenting now is different from what it was like in first-century Palestine.

A handful of observations might be helpful here. First, we should notice from the context that the lost, or prodigal, son is the last in a trilogy of parables about lost things. It belongs with the stories of the lost sheep and the lost coin. These parables aren't placed together by accident; the gospel writer means us to read them side-by-side. So, we ought to notice some of the differences between these parables and the similarity of theme. But here I want to mention just one difference: *value*. The missing sheep never loses its value; it never ceases to be a sheep. However daft it might be to risk 99 sheep for the sake of one, at least the one sheep is worth having! Likewise, the missing coin never loses value; it never becomes an ex-coin. But the dishonourable behaviour of the missing son towards the father renders him *valueless* in terms of the norms of that society.

Second, this means the younger son is socially dead; by the customary rules, he cannot be sought or found since he is no longer a son. We don't really think in terms of social death anymore. Social death is not the same as sending someone to Coventry; it is irrevocable. The relatively modern example of social death comes from the time when the death penalty was still legal. A condemned prisoner couldn't write a will. This is not because they weren't allowed, but rather because they were already dead in the eyes of the law, so it was impossible to write a will.

Third, the son's social death is a direct result of his behaviour; in effect, he refused to wait until the old man was dead before breaking his family ties of obligation and honour. The only honourable way forward for any father, however much he loved the boy, would be to accept his loss. Otherwise, he would lose face, and as the person in whom the identity and honour of the family resides, the father would not be free to do what he might like. The son knows this, too. This is why, when he returns, he intends to ask for work as a hired hand. He hopes to make it easier for the father to be merciful.

Fourth, we can now read the father's statement that the socially dead son 'is alive' (Luke 15:32) differently. This is not just extravagant language. The father really does mean what he says. This parable is about a social death being reversed. He was dead. He really was. But now he's alive. However, for any normal human father in this culture, this action could not occur without cost. According to the economy of finite honour, the son can be restored to life and value only by the father incorporating dishonour into himself.

Fifth, the economy of salvation here is, therefore, one of *transvaluation* – the reversal of life and death. It works *through* substitution and exchange. Just as the younger son performed 'reverse alchemy' on riches, turning them into ashes, now we have this reversed back. The prodigal son's death and dearth are converted back to a state of life and richness. At this point in the story, we begin to see the shadow of the cross; like the good shepherd in John's gospel, the father in this parable lays down his very self that his son may live again.

Sixth, *this* father displays a generosity far in excess of customary standards of ancient Mediterranean behaviour. He *needn't* have divided the property; he *needn't* have been on the lookout for the returning son; he *needn't* have run down the road; he *needn't* have restored the son to the family; he *needn't* have slaughtered the fatted calf in celebration of his son's rebirth. But he did. To be sure, this sort of behaviour would diminish a normal ancient Mediterranean father, but there is something about the constant generosity of *this* father that presses the analogy between God and us to its limits.

Seventh, God in this parable is no small god. God's capacity to be merciful and generous is directly proportionate to his honour, his glory – and this is infinite. Since, in the economy of infinite honour, he cannot be diminished by restoring us to life, he is not like a human father. Like this father, his love is free to be *endlessly* generous. The tragedy of the elder son is that he misses this and, regarding the father as disgraced through his profligacy and lack of judgement, he is emboldened to refuse the invitation to come into the feast.

Of course, there are other rich details in the parable. The father is insulted by both sons. The younger son is responsible for squandering the inheritance; the older is responsible for refusing to come and feast. A key part of the parable is the father's initiative in running to the son. Middle Eastern custom would have had the younger son met on the village's borders by an elder and a pot broken over the penitent's head as a sign of the irreparable damage that had been done to the village and to family honour. The father, in running, exposes his legs and makes haste. This is an undignified custom on the father's part, as elders do not run so much as glide or walk slowly as a sign of their dignity. It is for slaves, women and children to run, not for elders (compare Psalm 147:10).

The returning son would then have joined the servants. Any return to sonship would have had to be earned. The Greek text teases us a little with the potential for conflict at the end of the parable. In some translations, as the father runs to the son, the text tells us that 'he fell upon [the son's] neck' (v. 20). Interesting. The neck is vulnerable, breakable and exposed, but also sensitive. Until he is embraced, the son cannot know if he is about to be kissed – or frankly throttled.

But Jesus, as he so often does in parables, plays with our sense of fairness. Suppose your son or daughter 'borrowed' your credit card and ran up huge debts. To add to the fun, they had a wild party for several days while you were away. You come home with your partner to find the place trashed, many things sold or damaged, and a note from your child to say they have decided not to sit their A-levels but have instead bunked off to the Southeast Asia for an early taste of a gap year – or two. When your credit card bill arrives, you discover they have run up bills of tens of thousands of pounds. Your calls to their mobile phone are not returned, and they don't respond to emails.

But lo, two years later, your son or daughter rings up from Heathrow and says, 'Mum, Dad – I'm home…' What do you do? Do you [a] tell them to get the coach home – we'll talk later; [b] offer some repayment plans spread over several years and give them a severe dressing down; [c] say, 'We'll pick you up, and we're so glad to have you back that we're organising a lavish party at rather short notice.' Not c, I don't think.

But the justice of God is different. The parable of the prodigal plays with our sense of justice. And the older son hates it. The parable's message is this: the love of God is so complete as to be almost unjust – and certainly unfair. And this is why the party's event is so central to understanding the parable.

This excess is exuberance to the point of wastefulness. Indeed, many of the parables that Jesus tells are about things that are thrown away, used up or finished with. Whether it be a banquet that is eaten, the seed that is thrown around, or leaven which is baked with, Jesus' subjects, like Jesus himself, are used and then disposed of. A party that sets out to leave no waste is a very dull party. What marks the distinction between party time and the rest of our lives is this wastefulness; it is the expression of abundance, of blessing.

One more detail to draw our attention to is the tactile nature of this prodigal story – feet, tears, hair, sobbing and caressing. Simon Schama, in his excellent book *Through Rembrandt's Eyes*, deconstructs the famous painting *The Return of the Prodigal Son* in the light of the parable. In Rembrandt's picture, which hangs in St Petersburg, the older son hangs around in the shadows, looking on distantly and sternly at the scene. Schama, in a telling passage that resonates with the woman at the house of Simon, has this to say:

> The face of the sinner, the prodigal, whom Rembrandt had etched and drawn and painted before, once with the features of a Simian scapegrace, once with his own leering countenance, is turned away from us, his eyes shut, buried in the bosom of his forgiving father. Rembrandt's prodigal has been broken by his journey from

his transgression to atonement. The soles of his feet are lacerated and pierced, so that we understand that he has hobbled painfully home towards atonement. His finery hangs in pathetic rags and tatters from his emaciated frame. His head is shorn like a penitent's as he kneels in contrition. We can scarcely make out his features, so lightly has the artist drawn them, but we see enough to know this prodigal for Everyman, for the child who has taken all the sins of the world on his shoulders.[13]

Schama then moves his narrative to focus on the father, receiving the penitent:

The father, mantled in red, his brow shining with consummate peace, places his hands on those shoulders as if to lift the burden of his trespasses from them with his paternal blessing. But the gesture is even more than a rite of priestly healing: it is also an act of resurrection, a transformation of death into life. To the indignant righteous brother who protests against the fatted calf being killed for the prodigal, the father, God-like, retorts, 'this thy brother was dead, and is alive again'. So, the son kneels against the loins of the father, eyes shut, arms across his chest; they melt together in a single form, the pathetic shred of humanity returned to the boundlessly encompassing compassion of his creator.[14]

The shining brow infers the priestly oil of anointing, and not some sweat. This is a sign of gladness: 'Make your face shine on your servant' (Psalm 31: 16). We cannot see the face of the son, but the shining face of the father is one of infinite mercy, gladness and blessing. The face of God radiates that, just as Rembrandt's father's face does.

Rembrandt's portrait is an allegory. In much the same way, another story of a child trying to find their way home – L. Frank Baum's *The Wonderful Wizard of Oz* – is also an allegory. Perhaps it will surprise you that what is apparently a child's story was orginially a critique of American society and its appetite for 'gold rushes'. Thus, 'Oz' means ounce ('oz'), and the 'yellow brick road' is, as in the English folktale of

Dick Whittington ('the streets of London are paved with gold'), a road that lures the foolish and easily seduced, who in turn are represented by the scarecrow (poor rural farmers, needing sense), the tin man (greedy industrialists, needing heart), the lion (those lacking moral courage, needing strength) and Dorothy Gale (the gullible and innocent), to the 'holy grail of personal wealth'.

The 1939 film adaptation, *The Wizard of Oz* (produced by Mervyn LeRoy) reflects Baum's original allegory. When the party eventually reach Oz, the journey proves to have been worthless. The dreamy quality of the final song 'Over the rainbow' (the ballad written by Harold Arlen with lyrics by Yip Harburg) combines elements of lullaby and almost heavenly aspiration, a world where troubles 'melt away'. The song yearns for homecoming yet also puts the old world behind the singer: a new future now begins to open, one tinged with regret but also with promise.

We can make a few closing observations here about home, money and true riches. First, the film and the song have a strong 'prodigal' theme. Just as the character of Jesus' parable in Luke 15 decides to venture away from home, so do the characters in *The Wizard of Oz*, most especially Dorothy (whose name, incidentally, means 'gift from God').

Second, the resolution for restlessness and adventure is homecoming, with elements of repentance and forgiveness. The younger son might easily speak Dorothy's lines towards the close of the film of Jesus' parable: 'If I ever go looking for my heart's desire again, I won't look further than my own backyard, because if it isn't there, I never really lost it.'

Third, the morphic resonance of the prodigal theme takes on a life of its own within popular culture, which begins to exist independently of any religious reference. Elton John's song 'Goodbye yellow brick road' (co-written with Bernie Taupin), from the album of the same name, picks up where Dorothy left off. The religious origins in the song are opaque for most listeners, but they are present and powerful.

Indeed, the lyrics of 'Goodbye yellow brick road' represent a rather darker, more modern prodigal ballad. The young man in the song is unnamed but has been sucked into the high life as a 'rent boy' for a while and now finds himself cut adrift amid the low life. He longs for home. He's drinking heavily, lonely, miserable – and longing, like Dorothy, for the warmth of the farmstead he once knew, far from the bright lights. (Readers wondering about this reading of Elton John's song can listen to the B-side of the vinyl single, featuring the lesser-known song 'Screw you – young man's blues').

Ultimately, the parable of the prodigal son says that God's love remains total regardless of how lost we believe we are, how much we have squandered our lives or failed and no matter what burdens of shame we carry. There is nothing we can do to diminish our value to God (John 3:16). In God's eyes and heart, we are worth everything – and more.

Part 2
Counting the cost

7

Bureau de change

> In the temple he found those who were selling oxen and sheep
> and pigeons, and the money-changers sitting there. And making
> a whip of cords, he drove them all out of the temple, with the
> sheep and oxen. And he poured out the coins of the money-
> changers and overturned their tables. And he told those who
> sold the pigeons, 'Take these things away; do not make my
> Father's house a house of trade.' His disciples remembered that
> it was written, 'Zeal for your house will consume me.'
> JOHN 2:14–17

There's a telling moment in C.S. Lewis' *The Lion, the Witch and the
Wardrobe*, when the three children are introduced to Aslan. Aslan, let us
remember, is a lion. A big one. They eat meat. This could include other
animals – and children. When Aslan is being discussed in Mr Beaver's
house, Lucy, one of the children, asks rather anxiously, 'Is Aslan *safe*?'
Mr Beaver replies, 'Oh no, my dear, he's not *safe*; but he is *good*.' Can
you be good, but also pose serious threat? Yes. Nations manage this.
Communities too. I've even heard that parents manage it.

Although the story of Jesus clearing the temple features very early in the
gospel of John, other gospels link it inextricably to the events of Holy
Week, because it is an act of religious disturbance and violence that
points us towards the crucifixion itself. But there is some other background to this extraordinary gospel story, and there are other general
remarks to make here. Jesus is always dealing with small elite groups
who weaponise the law against others, either to exclude or denigrate
them or as a means of obtaining control, power and handsome profit.

This is what Jesus faces in the temple. He chooses not to argue with the merchants and the stallholders. Instead, he lays into them. For the avoidance of doubt, he thinks about this, and must realise that there will be some collateral damage. Some stallholders will know full well they are exploiting the poor and the gullible – taxing them before they can pray and worship. But some will, I am sure, think they are providing a genuine service: organic lambs, free-range pigeons – you get the idea. They will have pride in their products. Jesus does not discriminate. He lays into everyone.

Jesus also makes a whip of cords for this. It takes about three hours to make a good whip. Even if you are the Messiah, it still takes about three hours to make the same whip. Jesus, as a carpenter's boy, would have known how to use the tools, so he's had plenty of time to consider his actions and the consequences. He still went for it, and went in hard.

For sure, the other gospel writers spare us the details of the whip, but they are all clear that Jesus 'drives out' the merchants from the temple. This was not some polite 'Now, should you really be here, and would you like to think about relocating your stalls outside the temple precincts, please?' No. Jesus drove these people out. That was an action that required anger and menace. And while John puts this story early on in Jesus' ministry, it is undoubtedly an action – or sign – directly related to the actions taken against Jesus later, and leading to his arrest and execution. For Jesus, there will be no more 'business as usual' in the temple. Holy Week, Good Friday and Easter all proclaim that 'business has changed'. God is doing something different from now on, and the meltdown in the temple tells us there will be no going back.

Here are a couple of questions for our time. How do you love and care for a world that mostly enrages you, with all our political failures and social stigmatisation and deep social divisions? And how do you care for and love the church, which far from being that ark of salvation it is called to be, seems to enrage you even more? As the civil rights campaigner John Lewis said: 'There is never a wrong time to do the right thing.'

But is it ever right to be angry – even furious – at injustice? The gospels answer us: Yes. And John's account of Jesus cleansing the temple gives us some clues. Jesus is supposed to be a peaceable and wise teacher. But he creates mayhem in the temple and upsets all the people going about their lawful trading in dubious 'religious tat' and offerings.

The story in John's gospel is a meditation on Jesus' manifesting wisdom and also his alleged foolishness. Jesus spends much of his ministry being cast not as a hero, but as something of a loose cannon, and possibly even a deranged prophet. Thus his words and works are prejudged by his critics, because even in first-century Palestine, the social and theological construction of reality seems to prejudice many people's perceptions of Jesus.

To casual onlookers, turning out the traders from the temple is a foolish thing to do: they don't mean any harm, do they? Why pick on merchandisers selling 'religious tat', offerings and souvenirs? Or moneylenders, who we all have need of? We all accept this. Jesus, in contrast, does not; and as in other cases, behaves 'rather badly'. Behold! He eats and drinks with a bad crowd; he finds himself narrated as a glutton and a drunkard. So Jesus says, somewhat cryptically, that 'wisdom is justified by her deeds' (Matthew 11:19).

But there is a difference between hot anger and cold, perhaps righteous anger. Jesus actually went away and *made* the whip of cords he used on the hapless traders. This is not a rush of blood to the head. He has, as the epistle of James puts it, 'been slow to anger' (1:19) – but he's got there. And now he's meting out some prophetic discipline.

Wisdom is key. Because the second part of the gospel story outlines how the seemingly wise and righteous appear not to be able to see what is in front of their noses, while the apparently foolish and unrighteous seem to have perceived. So Jesus' action in the temple – reckless, violent and apparently intemperate – contains a radical, strong message. It conveys wisdom – which is that sometimes, breaking our frames of reference with such sharpness and anger is the only way to get people to see how foolish they have been.

This is the key to understanding the incident: it is about breaking a culture and smashing the prevailing frames of reference. Jesus never tolerates abusive cultures. So, Jesus is acting something out in this narrative: there was really no point at all in trading up from a pigeon to a dove. Neither sacrifice brings you closer to God; you are wasting your money. There is no point in going for the 'three-for-two' offer on goats or the 'buy-one-get-one-free' offer on lambs.

Much of the gospel of John is all about being reconciled to what has been hidden and looking deeper into what has been revealed. It is about seeing beyond the apparently obvious and finding the wisdom in apparent folly. This is why Jesus' anger in the gospel is so interesting in this story. It seems to not be a hot, quick irrational 'snap', but rather a cold, icy anger.

Rather like Arnie (a robot from the future) in the film *The Terminator*, Jesus has seen the temple and said to his audience: 'I'll be back.' As Harvey Cox writes, the first and original sin is not disobedience; it is, rather, indifference.[15] We can no longer ignore the pain and alienation that others in the church experience – especially when this is *because* of the church. Indifference is pitiful, and it is the enemy of compassion.

Jesus had to reject the religious elites of his day, because they had taken possession of the law and tradition, its meanings and applications. We have an old saying: 'Possession is nine-tenths of the law.' By claiming ownership of faith, religion and morality, the religious elites of Jesus' time were able to remain aloof. These religious leaders could issue edicts. They could decide if and when they went into 'dialogue', and with whom.

Most difficult questions could be left unanswered, and difficult questioners were censured and censored. By purloining religion – in theory to protect it, but in the end to possess it – the religious elites of Jesus' day were able put themselves above others. The elite were not like the people. These leaders could not be weighed, cross-examined, investigated, inspected or judged. Anyone who joined this elite acquired power and privilege, with immunity from accountability.

Jesus, by walking with the poor and outcast, befriending them as valued equals in the kingdom of heaven, simply destroyed the wall that prevented them from coming close to God. Remember Jesus' words in Matthew 18:6–7 – 'Whoever causes one of these little ones… to sin, it would be better for him to have a great millstone fastened round his neck and to be drowned in the depth of the sea. Woe to the world for temptations to sin! For it is necessary that temptations come, but woe to the one by whom the temptation comes!'

On the face of it, the issue of causing others to stumble into sin is apparently a 'tripping point'. Romans 14:13 bears that out: 'Let us not pass judgement on one another any longer, but rather decide never to put a stumbling block or hindrance in the way of [another].' Yet a millstone around your neck is a pretty heavy block. However, our term 'stumbling block' is not what it seems. It comes from the Greek word *skandalon* (used 15 times in the New Testament) and is the source of our word *'scandal'*. The related verb ('to cause to stumble') is *skandalizō* (used 30 times in the New Testament), from which we get 'scandalise'.

To us, a scandal is just toxic gossip and tabloid tittle-tattle – and might summon memories of some celebrity libel trial or more serious courtroom drama involving loss of life, or some failure of government. However, to the ancient Greeks, a scandal was the functional trigger mechanism for a baited trap. Later, it came to mean the actual trap, or something that tripped a person up, causing them to stumble and fall. In the Bible, a stumbling block is anything that causes a person to fall – be that into sin, false teaching or unbelief.

But there is another side to this. Jesus Christ was a *skandalon*: 'We preach Christ crucified, a stumbling block to Jews and folly to Gentiles' (1 Corinthians 1:23). The late Pope Francis argued that the merciful response to the corrupt is to place a stumbling block, a *skandalon*, in their path, which is the only way of forcing them to seriously contemplate taking a different road. One thinks of the rich man who obeys all the law and excels at good works. What else is he to do? A *skandalon* is placed before him: 'Jesus said to him, "If you would be perfect, go, sell what you possess and give to the poor, and you will have treasure in heaven; and come, follow me." When the young man heard this he went away sorrowful, for he had great possessions' (Matthew 19:21–22).

As Francis observed, Jesus does cure the corrupt – not through acts of mercy, but rather through engineering major trials and the deliberate infliction of disturbing trauma. In Luke 8, Jairus is made to wait for Jesus to heal his daughter. Jesus, running late, and quite deliberately so, does nothing to prevent her untimely death. But in the act of healing the woman with continuous menstrual bleeding, he enables her to participate in synagogue worship once again. She is healed. Her stigmatisation is taken away by Jesus' touch. No longer impure, she has her status restored.

Jairus, a synagogue ruler, would have been instrumental in excluding this woman from such worship. The healing of the woman, and the raising of Jairus' daughter, is both a blessing and a trauma for Jairus. It is bitter-sweet. For Jairus must now face the culture of exclusion he was instrumental in upholding. He must face this woman. To get Jairus to this point, he is, arguably, made to lose and grieve for his daughter. She dies. The moral lesson of the miracle lies in the judgement it makes against the culture of exclusion in ritual purity. Only when the culture is exposed to trauma can it change. Jairus may now repent of his participation in decades of structural oppression. But it is only the trauma of his daughter's loss that got him there.

Such traumas have the potential to pierce the armour of corruption and allow grace to enter. To treat faith as a suit of armour – a means of self-defence – is to deny the possibility of God surprising us with amazing grace, the compassion of the stranger and the revelation of Christ in the prisoner, hungry, sick and homeless. If we encase ourselves in our own armoured-personal faith, we will only mummify ourselves. But never enough, so our body soon degrades and decomposes. The body that we armour too tightly becomes pallid, compromised, corrupted – and eventually stinks.

Throughout the gospels, we see Jesus *not* forgiving the sins of the scribes, Pharisees and Sadducees. Their culture is an indicator of a religion that regards itself as morally self-sufficient and superior to others. Jesus' caustic castigations – straining gnats while swallowing camels or picking out specks in someone else's eye when there is a plank in your own – are *unforgiving*.

Those who are corrupt will always try to justify themselves with comparisons to others. The parable of the Pharisee and the tax collector in Luke 18 comes to mind, with its hints of smug triumphalism. In the parable the latter articulates not only their guilt, but also their sense of shame. In contrast, the corrupt will usually be shamelessly and morally smug. The agents of this culture of corruption can easily recruit more accomplices, as they are offering them an experience of graduation into moral-spiritual superiority, self-satisfaction and self-sufficiency. This culture eats all nascent initiatives designed to correct it. In the end, it will of course consume itself.

So, we are back with the necessity of creative rage and constructive destruction. Why? Because the offer of dialogue by those remaining in power can never heal corruption. The only way to deal with corruption is to cause the powerful serious trials, tribulations and traumas, so that grace can finally break through, light pierce the fog of bureaucracy and the wind of the Spirit scatter the secrets shrouded in darkness.

Jesus acts this out in the temple, driving away the money-changers and sellers on the stalls. This first-century Jerusalem bureau de change now assumes a new identity. Jesus' actions say there is nothing you can exchange for God's free love and mercy. You cannot purchase it. Nor can you buy your way into heaven for a better seat or a position closer to God. No taxes, interest rates or hidden extras apply to God's love, generosity, grace and abundance. This encounter in the temple, therefore, presents us with everything Jesus will stand against. The only valid currencies in the temple are love, justice, mercy and truth. There are no tokens or offerings that can make up for the loss or absence.

There are three more things to say in relation to Jesus' emotional temperament here. First, what is Jesus so upset about in the temple? It seems to me that it lies in assumptions: about the 'natural order of things'; about status and privilege; about possessions; about prevailing wisdom. This is about, in other words, unexamined lives and practices lived in unexamined contexts. Everyone is blind. Jesus' action forces us to confront the futile sight before us. His cold blazing anger forces us to look again.[16]

Second, the story chides us all for that most simple of venial sins: overlooking. The trading has been happening for years and years. It is simply part of the furniture; it barely merits a look, let alone comment. Jesus, of course, always looks deeper. But the lesson of the story is that, having looked into us with such penetration, his gaze then often shifts – to those who are below us, and unseen. That is, those with less wealth, health, intelligence, conversation and social skills, or just less life.

Third, the besetting sin is that the temple traders accept the status quo. The story has one thing to say about this: *Don't*. Don't accept that a simple small gesture cannot ripple out and begin to change things. Don't accept, wearily, that you can't make a difference. You can.

Sometimes the change may be radical, but more often than not, change comes about through small degrees. Reform can be glacial and adaptationist. We need to stop waiting and start acting. Nigel Biggar writes that:

> True prophets are ones who don't much enjoy playing prophet. They don't enjoy alienating people, as speakers of uncomfortable truths tend to do. They don't enjoy the sound of their own

solitary righteousness and they don't enjoy being in a minority of one. True prophets tend to find the whole business irksome and painful. They want to wriggle out of it, and they only take to it with reluctance. So beware of those who take to prophesy like a duck to water, and who revel in the role. They probably aren't the real thing.[17]

True prophets can be thoughtful, kind and cautious creatures. And angry. Caricatures of raging fire-storming preachers should be set aside. True prophets are more emotionally integrated. They are pastoral, contextual and political theologians. They care about people and places. They have virtues such as compassion, care, kindness, self-control, humility and gentleness. But they have passion and energy for change too, often reluctantly expressed, and only occasionally finding voice in anger. Pure compassion can be quite ruthless. (Ask any parent who loves their child.)

The scandal of our churches and church leaders is that they prefer to survive rather than be true; they choose optics over justice; they privilege pride and reputation over honesty and integrity. To Jesus, this is a scandal. To the world, it is a scandal. To emerging generations, it means the church is bound to a lengthy sojourn in the wilderness of ever-increasing indifference. This gospel asks us to think hard about how we channel our anger about injustice. Start with the church, even though some will call you mad or drunk for doing so.

Feminist theologians remind us that some anger is good. Passion can be furious and still good. But what we feel, sometimes, is a sense of personal hurt, not moral injustice. The moral question is not, 'How or what do I feel?', but rather, 'What should I do with these feelings?' Often, the answer is peace, not prosecution, let alone violence. But sometimes, the only response to injustice is righteous anger. Not just shouting and raging, but acting the anger out: 'Let the reader understand' (Mark 13:14).

8

The price of oil

> One of the Pharisees asked him to eat with him, and he went
> into the Pharisee's house and took his place at the table. And
> behold, a woman of the city, who was a sinner, when she learned
> that he was reclining at table in the Pharisee's house, brought
> an alabaster flask of ointment, and standing behind him at
> his feet, weeping, she began to wet his feet with her tears and
> wiped them with the hair of her head and kissed his feet and
> anointed them with the ointment. Now when the Pharisee who
> had invited him saw this, he said to himself, 'If this man were a
> prophet, he would have known who and what sort of woman
> this is who is touching him, for she is a sinner.'
>
> LUKE 7:36–50

Luke's story of the anointing does not fall in his account of Holy Week.
But the reading, for good reasons, as we shall see, does come in the
Holy Week readings under the *Revised Common Lectionary* for the
Chrism Eucharist. One way of tackling parables is to resort to the
allegorical tradition that was so beloved by early Christian writers and
Jewish scholars. John's gospel lends itself particularly well to this treatment – especially the 'signs' of Jesus. But here, I have chosen to read
a familiar passage from Luke as a parable. The story is of the woman
who anoints the feet of Jesus at the house of Simon the Pharisee (Mark
calls him 'Simon the Leper'). Jesus responds to the incident – a parable
within a parable – by telling the story of the two debtors. The narrative
concludes with the woman having her sins forgiven, about which she
has said nothing, let alone made a confession.

The story reminds me of the retelling of the story of the woman caught in adultery by the writer and poet Andrew Hudgins. Jesus walks into town one day and encounters a disturbing crowd scene: a group of men gathered around a woman, threatening her with stones. Jesus walks into the centre of the angry mob, looks them all in the eye, and says: 'Ye who is without sin may cast the first stone.' No one moves a muscle. Then gradually, one by one, all begin to melt away.

Jesus is about to turn to the woman, tell her to 'go and sin no more', when from the back of the crowd, someone lobs an enormous brick. It sails through the air, and with brilliant accuracy, hits the woman caught in adultery on the head, knocking her cold to the ground. 'Who threw that?' Jesus asks sternly. No one moves again. 'I say again,' says Jesus, 'who threw that?' Still, no one owns up. Jesus is about to get angry when he sees a little face at the back of the crowd, and he recognises it. 'Oh, Mother,' he says, 'do go home.'[18]

This story is obviously about sin and forgiveness, and who deserves to be absolved. It makes the point that we all sin, some more than others, but it is sin nonetheless. Therefore, no one ought to be too proud; neither should anyone be too ashamed. But it is also about a great deal more than that. Simon, it seems, was unsure about the status of his guest. He respected him enough to call him 'Teacher', but failed to offer Jesus any of the usual courtesies that betokened warmth: no perfume, footbath or kiss – it was a rather formal, stilted, even sterile atmosphere. And so, we are presented with the shock in the narrative: an unnamed woman treats Jesus with more respect and warmth than the religious and wise host, who ought to know better. So, who is really wise? Who is gracious? Not Simon.

The irony of this story is that a 'rude' intruder shows the civilised how to behave properly. You can almost sense the 'tutting' eyes as the woman walks in, the whispers behind hands, 'What's *she* doing here?', almost as though a homeless person had tried to sit at the high table. We have no reason to suppose that the woman knew Jesus person-ally, but she knows enough of his reputation as a healer, teacher and person of compassion to come to the meal. Yet the encounter turns into something deeply complex and challenging.

Jesus tells us that in the face of the prisoner (sinner), naked, poor and hungry we meet God: 'Truly, I say to you, as you did it to one of the least of these my brothers, you did it to me' (Matthew 25:40). Perhaps Luke portrays the woman as an *ikon* of God – a trinitarian one at that – to subvert the false pride of Simon and his guests.

Like the *Father*, the woman takes the initiative, a bold feature of this story. She comes to Jesus as God comes to us: she is a revelation. It is not that Jesus finds her; she seeks him. Jesus is being 'lost' in this meal, and the woman's offering places him at the centre again. Yet the action of the woman will also call for a response, not just from Jesus, but from all the guests. Here is an epiphany, yet not a moment that demands obedience: all are free to respond – no one is forced.

Like *Jesus*, she also serves, 'taking the form of a servant' (Philippians 2:7). There are echoes of the foot-washing of the disciples in John 13 – there is a sacramental quality here. The whole ridiculous hierarchy of the meal is subverted by this act of service: 'I am among you as the one who serves' (Luke 22:27).

We don't know why she sinned or necessarily even how – it was probably prostitution. But does it matter? No, because she puts any pride she has behind her and gets on with giving herself in humility and strength. Like the *Holy Spirit*, she is poured out in oil and in tears, anointing the Son: 'This is my beloved Son, with whom I am well pleased' (Matthew 3:17). She settles on him, brooding over him like creation, giving of herself. The kisses are a seal; she is the giving gift of God. Here is true *kenosis* – self-emptying for the other. The whole event is a Christophany: Jesus and the woman mirroring each other in dynamic relationality.

It is perhaps a bit tendentious to suggest that in the face of a woman of ill-repute we meet an *ikon* of God. Yet the double shock of the story is that Jesus lets himself be ministered to in this way. Simon would have flinched from the contamination; Jesus allows himself to be caressed by it. In this woman, we do meet God.

God is indeed embodied in the most surprising places – alive and well in the sick, the oppressed, the God-forsaken... not just the learned and the holy. What the story is starting to show us is that the power–powerless axis is a key to the story. Simon is the host with power, but he will not stoop to welcome Jesus properly. The woman is clearly powerless, yet she will lay aside her last sediments of power to embrace her healing and to admit her need of Jesus. She is empowered; Simon is disempowered.

If it is true that pride comes before a fall, then you might think that the trick is to keep the pride but watch your step. Yet the *art* with pride is to remember that we are fallen first in God's eyes: we started from the ground. There is a wonderful Fijian proverb that is used to deflate the powerful who appear to get above themselves: 'The higher up the tree the monkey climbs, the more you see its bottom'. It reminds us, as Simon and his guests appeared to have forgotten, that we are all human and equal before God. Only from that position of humility can we experience the grace to stand tall for ourselves, the other and for God.

The anointing at Bethany was enormously significant according to Jesus, though I suspect his disciples saw it as an irksome intrusion. Yet Jesus knew this incident to be one that formed a core part of the gospel. Theologians call this incident a *kerygma*: 'Truly, I say to you, wherever this gospel is proclaimed in the whole world, what she has done will also be told in memory of her' (Matthew 26:13).

It is no accident these the words are like what Jesus himself said about the Eucharist: 'Do this in memory of me.' It is ironic, is it not? We celebrate the Eucharist daily, but the anointing at Bethany? Never. The words 'Messiah' (Hebrew) and 'Christ' (Greek) simply mean 'the Anointed One"' and, in the Psalms, 'the Lord's Anointed' refers to the king who will usher in God's reign.

Theology, being largely a male preserve for most of its two thousand years, would prefer you to believe that Jesus is anointed and commissioned at his baptism by John, and witnessed to by the Holy Spirit. Yet this moment – when Jesus is anointed – is in all four gospels. This should alert us to its importance. The same can only be said of the most crucial events: his baptism, the miraculous feedings, his passion and resurrection.

Across the four gospels, different emphases in narrative and purpose are bound to emerge as each evangelist seeks to give us a distinctive portrayal of the life and work of Jesus. Thus, one gospel might take the anointing as an anticipation of the burial of Jesus. A different gospel might focus on the woman and her outpouring of love and gratitude mixed with agonised grief for his coming death. Equally, another gospel can take the anointing as really belonging to the events leading to the Passover and the betrayal, trial and death of Jesus. Only Luke places his description of the anointing this early in the ministry of Jesus.

Each gospel is like a portrait, and perhaps it is best to think of them as complex oil paintings with hundreds of figures and scenes on one giant canvas. It is not that one portrait or gospel is better than the others, let alone that one is more accurate than the other. These are like paintings – beautiful portraits of real people, events and situations in real time, but committed to a canvas and frame that inevitably gives us something different every time we look, let alone compared to other portraits. The gospels are dynamic and rich in what they portray, and the inevitable differences in emphasis and narrative stress do not infer that one is right and others wrong. That is not how art, history and literature work. The gospels are no different. They are the medium God has chosen to speak of the life of Jesus. The differences in the gospels are but one example of the rich tapestry we encounter through God's revelation.

As we consider the price of oil in the story of the anointing, we are also invited to work backwards to the gifts brought by the Magi at the birth of Jesus. When the wise men came to visit, they brought quite expensive gifts – gold, frankincense and myrrh have never been cheap. The word 'epiphany' simply means 'manifestation', and the gifts from the wise men are traditionally the culmination of the early manifestation of Jesus' divinity. (This is also redolent of the account of Jesus' anointing.) So just as the wise men from the east bring gifts fit for a king, now we have the oil of anointing and burial. The richness of the scent and the sheer expense of the gesture nudges the reader forward to Jesus' kingship, but also to his burial and the sacrificial, costly and ritual treatment of a dead body.

The cost of such gestures is a concern. Many of our true radicals – some would say wise men – have understood that God discriminates for the poor, and that Christianity must question its comfortable roots to be truly incarnational. The early church needed money, but they also knew how to give it away. The early Christian socialists worked with Chartists, radicals and other organisations to bring justice for the working class. They argued for universal suffrage, set up colleges and cooperatives, and laboured for the labourer. They saw that God was for the poor, that God had made a resolution – a covenant, if you will – that the church was for all.

As T.S. Eliot in 'Journey of the Magi' reminds us: this journey was costly. Yet there was no immediate comfort at the end of that. What they found instead was something more familiar to our society: an ordinary family, in temporary accommodation, struggling with a new baby. It must have been quite a shock: they had tried Herod's palace first, but found they got the wrong address. Yet the gospel records that they still gave their gifts, expensive as they were, and left them at the poor and lowly stable.

In their own way, the wise men were quite radical, and they throw a question back to us. What gifts will we give to the homeless, the displaced, the poor and the marginalised? This question isn't a political party matter: it is a spiritual, moral and social matter. Our response to this story might turn out to be costly too. This is discipleship. That's why I especially like this prayer that marks the birth of Jesus and Epiphany:

Thank you
scandalous God,
for giving yourself to the world
not in the powerful and extraordinary
but in weakness and the familiar:
in a baby; in bread and wine.

Thank you
for offering, at journey's end, a new beginning;
for setting, in the poverty of stable,
the richest jewel of your love;
for revealing, in a particular place,
your light for all nations…

Thank you
for bringing us to Bethlehem, House of Bread,
where the empty are filled,
and the filled are emptied;
where the poor find riches,
and the rich recognize their poverty;
where all who kneel and hold out their hands
are unstintingly fed.[19]

But to return to Luke's story, other differences in the anointing of Jesus can be noted here. In Matthew 26 and Mark 14 the woman pours oil on the head of Jesus. In Luke 7 and John 12, the woman anoints Jesus on the feet and wipes the oil with her hair, in a way that stresses the sensuous nature of the encounter, and physicality of this gesture and powerful emotions of love and gratitude.

Perhaps John has Jesus' feet being anointed as a prelude to his charge to his disciples to wash one another's feet (John 13)? Taken as a whole, the gospels witness to the huge quantity and expense of the perfumed oil, the words of Jesus about the poor being 'always with you' and the anointing being a preparation for his burial. Mark and John share the detail of the value being 300 denarii, the indignation of the onlookers and Jesus' firm defence of the woman's behaviour. For these and other reasons, most commentators, though not all, consider that we have four versions of the same event.

Broadly, I agree. But then there is this question: who is the woman who anoints Jesus? I think she is Mary, the sister of Martha and of Lazarus, whom Jesus raised from the dead. She is named in John 12:1–8 as Mary of Bethany. The feminist theologian Elisabeth Schüssler Fiorenza has hypothesised that her name may have been omitted in the other gospels precisely because she was a woman.

A more charitable interpretation comes from the English theologian Richard Bauckham, who suggests that she was being granted 'protective anonymity'. It is certainly plausible that any woman acknowledging or even designating Jesus as the royal Messiah might have placed her in danger, were she identified as having been complicit in Jesus' politically subversive claim to messianic kingship. Protecting the earliest Christian communities may have led the gospel writers to redact many of the known names of people Jesus met with and healed. We hardly ever learn the name of any of these people, and often only might know them through ranking – such as Jairus' daughter or the centurion's boy-slave. The German theologian Elisabeth Moltmann-Wendel was a clear advocate of this hypothesis, taking the view that just as the prophet Samuel anointed Saul (and later David) as king, pouring a flask of oil on his head, so 'the unknown woman is at the same time a prophet who anoints the Messiah, consecrates him and equips him for his task'.[20]

More recently, there has been something of a small explosion of interest in Jesus' anointing. For example, in 1994, new work emerged claiming Bethany as a messianic anointing. The Japanese biblical scholar Hisako Kinukawa's *Women and Jesus in Mark* and Marianne Sawicki's *Seeing the Lord* affirm that the anointing of Jesus is what confers his messianic nature and his Christological identity. More recently, the Jesuit biblical translator Nicholas King, my good friend and neighbour, has stated that 'an unknown woman is anointing Jesus as Messiah', and Jesus is explaining (to onlookers) 'that she is anointing him for burial (so it is a dying Messiah)'.[21]

The account of the anointing in Luke 7 often leads commentators to assume that the woman is Mary Magdalene. I doubt this very much and am drawn to the idea that, where possible, characters interacting with Jesus were given deliberate 'protective anonymity'. While that may have been appropriate for the early Christians, seeking as they did to usher in the kingdom of God, our time is different. It is time to consciously name and own the women around Jesus, and perhaps especially Mary of Bethany, as her anointing of Jesus is key to his messianic claims and to her recognition of who he is as the Christ.

Even taking the narrative in Luke 7 at face value, I think we can detect the hand of a gospel writer who knew how to manage Mary's 'protective anonymity'. At the same time, it gives us rich and deep insights into what this moment meant. The woman who anoints the feet of Jesus, like the mother of Jesus, recognised who he was, even before the breaking of the bread and before the resurrection. Mary of Bethany is a prophet, servant, sage and priest. She is *kerygma* and Christophany. She paid for the oil. She poured out the oil. She anointed Jesus. She is the gift and the giver. As Jesus says, what Mary of Bethany has done 'will be told in memory of her'. I have only re-told this.

9

The currency of love

> Jesus, knowing that the Father had given all things into his hands, and that he had come from God and was going back to God, rose from supper. He laid aside his outer garments, and taking a towel, tied it round his waist. Then he poured water into a basin and began to wash the disciples' feet and to wipe them with the towel that was wrapped round him.
>
> JOHN 13:1–17

Recently, I have been trying to learn some conversational Cantonese. It is not an easy language – at least nine different tones to get your head around, a different way of moving your mouth and tongue, and even breathing – but I am trying my best.

What do you think is the third most used language in the USA, behind English and Spanish? It is not Chinese, Italian or German, although German was until around 1800 the second most spoken language in the USA. The answer is American Sign Language (ASL).

During the Covid-19 lockdowns, many people baked bread or watched Netflix. Others, like 17-year-old Mariella Satow, spent their time changing the world! Mariella has dual citizenship in the USA and the UK. At the start of the pandemic, she happened to be in New York and couldn't leave due to travel restrictions.

Getting up at dawn to go to online school back in England meant she had a lot of free time in the afternoons, so she decided to learn American Sign Language (ASL), one of 300 worldwide sign languages. The teenager thought seeing an ASL interpreter in action might help her learn faster, but when she looked up movies and TV shows on streaming platforms, she discovered they didn't use ASL interpreters. They may offer closed captioning or audio description but no ASL. Mariella decided there and then to change that!

She created an app that uses a simple Google Chrome extension. It adds an ASL interpreter to the corner of movies so people who are deaf or partially deaf can watch both simultaneously. The teen decided to focus her efforts first on the Disney+ platform because that's what she thought children watch the most.

Broadcasters and platform streaming companies said you can just turn on the subtitles. However, sign language includes face, hands, arms and body language. Captions and subtitles give you no emotion. They cannot tell you what the background noise is. They cannot offer emotional literacy. They cannot convey or show love – only read it out. Creating the Sign-Up App took her about a year to complete. She sought help from ASL teachers and the deaf community along the way, producing a sleek app that is already making kids and parents very happy.

One parent said, 'Seeing my son be able to sit and understand the movie and see things he's not seen before in eight years, it's amazing... We have captions, but they don't really do anything for him because it goes quite fast. He would just watch and not get much from it.' This creates a level playing field for kids like his son. He continued, 'Kids are getting that understanding and information like any hearing child does — they learn a language even before they go to school.'[22]

As I often remark, Jesus is the 'body language of God' — God's sign language to us. Jesus hears the unheard, sees the unseen, embraces the unfelt and neglected, holds the rejected and speaks for those not spoken for.

The *ouroboros* is an ancient symbol of a snake eating its own tail. The image is often found in jewellery, but also figures in illustrated manuscripts and art. The earliest known *ouroboros* is found in ancient Egypt, but it made its way into esoteric Christian thinking via ancient Greece. The word derives from the ancient Greek *oura* ('tail') and *boros* ('eating'). Sometimes the symbol has positive connotations associated with renewal. But equally, the symbol can also infer self-consumption and point to decline. Eating yourself to stave off hunger only goes one way and leads to one end.

In some ways, the symbol of the *ouroboros* presents us with a perfect paradigm for the church of today. How does the church fund its mission and ministry? By feeding off itself and consuming more of its own human and economic resources to maintain its mass. How does it fill itself again? By taking from another part of the church. This is self-mutilation in the service of self-preservation.

The early church was not concerned with self-preservation. The first martyrdom of the book of Acts – that of Stephen – shows that costly acts of service may lead to death rather than the gratitude of spectators. The early church followed the example of Jesus with a new currency of love, namely that of service. But these are forms of service usually left to those who have no reputation or status to lose. Jesus' washing of the disciples' feet is the responsibility of the host – a token gesture – but is bound to be delegated to a slave or servant. Jesus, in taking on the role, takes the lowest social position possible. Service, like love, is action, not just words.

In our present age, the lowest-paid jobs, irrespective of qualifications, are often taken by migrants, refugees and asylum seekers. In my own city, Aberdeen, I frequently meet people from Africa, the Middle East, South America and Eastern Europe who, in their own land, were doctors and dentists, architects, educators or who held some other skilled profession. In the UK, however, they work as carers and cleaners in care homes for the elderly or have taken on manual labour. Their service and value are beyond question, but as in the story of the foot washing, they have set aside their status. What makes the story of Jesus' action so revolutionary is his validation and sacralisation of service, irrespective of status. In God's economy, all are equal. So, all must learn to serve. This cannot be delegated to a third party, let alone to a slave or servant. It is what the *host* does (pun intended).

We see something of this legacy in the miraculous raising of Dorcas (Acts 9). The miracle occurs in Joppa – modern-day Jaffa – and on an important trade route for silks, spices and other merchandise that connects Asia Minor to Egypt and Arabia. Dorcas is a significant woman of accomplishment. She is a tailor, seamstress and clothing manufacturer. We learn she uses her wealth and virtue for charity and other good works. Like Lydia of Thyatira, a merchant in purple cloth and dye and the leader of the Philippian church, Dorcas stands in a strong tradition of entrepreneurial women who are converts to Christianity and key leaders in the early church. So, Dorcas' death was a grievous loss.

The name Dorcas (or Tabitha) is also notable. It means 'gazelle' – lively, sprightly, strong, fast and able. And she's a disciple too. This explains the throwaway at the end of the miracle story. Peter calls 'the saints and widows' together to show them Dorcas is alive (Acts 9:41). Why mention 'widows' as a category? Because the early church cared for the orphans and the widows, whether they were believers or not. This early church – the body language of God – looked out for and looked after those whom society did not care for. It is safe to assume that Dorcas used her wealth to support those without aid.

So, how are Christians supposed to engage with the world when they are, in truth, expecting a new world that is yet to come? Why bother with menial acts of service in the temporal sphere when minds and hearts are meant to be fixed on the eternal realm? These questions pepper the pages of the New Testament and have absorbed Christians for two millennia.

On the one hand, Christians are called out of the world and are to no longer regard themselves as belonging to it. On the other hand, they are to be engaged with the world in all its complexities and ambiguities as fully as possible, being salt, light and least in society, incarnating the life of Christ into the hubris of humanity. Money and the economy remain central concerns of social and public life, not just at national levels, but also as one of the defining issues of international affairs and global issues. Major Christian concerns are how to view debt, how to create and share wealth, and what our responsibilities are to the poor. Make no mistake: money matters.

To be sure, the ministry of Jesus was inherently political and economic in character as much as it was 'other-worldly'. This had profound implications for how Christians imagined the new world order. The gospel of John presents the reader with a Christ who calls Christians out of the world, but at the same time leaves them in it (e.g. John 15:19; 17:14; 18:36). In the same way, the radical words and actions of Jesus appear (at first sight) to point in opposite directions. Yet to only understand Jesus as a radical interferer within the social order of first-century Palestine would be to ignore another dimension of his agenda: the kingdom of God, which is to come. The radical discipleship demanded by Jesus may be said to dwell less on reform and more on revolution. Employment and families are to be forsaken for the kingdom – the ushering in of the new reign of God. Even the dead can be left unburied (e.g. Matthew 8:22; Luke 9:57–62).

Moreover, the disciples are not to anticipate reward or rule in this life; all recognition of costly service and devotion is postponed until the *eschaton*, where the wheat will be separated from the chaff and the righteous rewarded (Matthew 6:19–21). In very early Christian tradition, the apparent imminence of the kingdom of God led some to give up work and others to lead a life of celibacy. But by the time the later documents of the New Testament were being written, Christians were being urged to respect and work with temporal authorities, get on with their ordinary labours, live and earn responsibly, and begin to apply gospel principles to this life rather than speculating about the actual date of the *parousia*.

These two distinct traditions within early Christian teaching are closely related. Each act of service (e.g. hospitality, charity), each extension of costly love (e.g. of turning the other cheek, loving your enemies) and each vicarious sacrifice points towards the kingdom that is to come. Within Christian tradition, the kingdom is the place where society is reordered: the poor are made rich, captives are liberated, the lame walk and the blind are restored to sight (Luke 4:18–19). It is also the place where the impoverished inherit the kingdom, the mourners are comforted, the meek and the peacemakers are rewarded, and the persecuted are redeemed (Matthew 5:3–11). In other words, Christian social teaching anticipates the rule of God in prayer and action: 'Your kingdom come, your will be done, on earth as it is in heaven' (Matthew 6:10).

This tradition and teaching are reflected in the very first Christian communities. Stephen, the first Christian martyr, was a deacon with special responsibility for the daily distribution of alms to widows and orphans (Acts 6:1–3), reflecting the commitment to charity and service that is advocated in the gospels. In character, the first churches, although diverse in practice and belief, appear nevertheless to have exhibited a radical openness to questions of parity and inclusion. The original spirit of St Stephen's Day is caught in J.M. Neale's famous 19th-century carol, celebrating Wenceslas as he tracks down an unknown beggar in a snowstorm to give him a feast. The carol ends with a moral warning:

Therefore, Christians all, be sure,
Wealth or rank possessing,
Ye who now will bless the poor,
Shall yourselves find blessing.

This is the very antithesis of the *ouroboros*. It is in giving that we receive, not in consuming. It is by blessing others, not ourselves, that we discover the hand and heart of God. The currency of God's love is only for giving away. It is not for hoarding to ourselves.

So, what are Christians to be about in a world dominated by market forces and economic issues? The term for 'church' is the simple Greek word *ekklesia*, meaning the 'assembly of the people' who belong to but are called out of their community. All over the Mediterranean world, assemblies determined the politics, polity and civic ordering of communities and cities. But they were usually only open to citizens, and the power to speak and vote was normally confined to men.

The assemblies of the New Testament church – the deliberate adoption of the more internationalist term must have caused confusion to potential converts, as well as making a point – were, in contrast, inclusive. In these *ekklesia*, women were admitted, as were slaves, children, foreigners and other visitors. In other words, the character of the New Testament *ekklesia* represented and embodied a different kind of spiritual and social ordering that eschewed discrimination on grounds of race, gender and other criteria.

Christianity was, from the outset, an inherently political, economically active and profoundly social faith. A vivid and righteous expression of Christian faith will always challenge the present world order. Yet it is, at the same time, prepared to work within it, regarding nothing as being beyond redemption. Acts of costly service are what we are called to.

So, what is God's sign language in foot-washing here? Of course, it is a sign of service, humility and becoming a servant. Foot-washing is alien to our society as a gesture of service, but there is an activity closer to our public memory. Shoeshiners on street corners were once commonplace in our cities. For a few pennies, someone would stoop at your feet and buff up your brogues. There was often conversation and rapport with the shoeshiner, but fundamentally this was an act of service, albeit paid. To clean shoes like this publicly required humility. Or maybe it needed more than that – to acknowledge that you had no power, few possessions and no position.

Seeing Jesus' foot-washing at the last supper in this light starts to get near the centre of his gesture. He washes his disciples' feet because the events of Holy Week have gradually stripped him of his power and status as a teacher and healer. His ritual is an enactment of just how low he has sunk. So, he is a servant at the table: his face is focused on his feet, his eyes cast low. Even then, the darkness of Good Friday is already upon him. And now, today, he is stripped of everything, and he will sink even lower and into death itself.

Yet strangely, Jesus is also setting an example for his disciples. In John's gospel, foot-washing is a gesture of deep and abiding friend-ship and citizenship: 'You also ought to wash one another's feet' (John 13:14). This is a final reminder from Jesus to his disciples: service is the hallmark of a genuine community and faith in Christ. Just as the poor will inherit the kingdom of heaven, so will the church be led by the servants of the servants.

Decades later, after this encounter at the last supper, Paul recites an early Christian hymn in his letter to the Philippians:

> Christ Jesus, who, though he was in the form of God, did not count equality with God a thing to be grasped, but made himself nothing, taking the form of a servant, being born in the likeness of men. And being found in human form, he humbled himself by becoming obedient to the point of death, even death on a cross.
> PHILIPPIANS 2:5–8

The sign we encounter on Good Friday is the sign of the cross, and it is closely linked to the love and service we see on Maundy Thursday. Today is about learning to sign our lives in love, as Christ does; to serve, as Christ does; to be the body language of God and full of God's love, as Christ is. We can learn any language we like, but love is the only one that matters.

The cross is the ultimate sign of love. As one ancient English writer said several hundred years ago to help us remember:

We are so preciously loved by God that we cannot even comprehend it. No created being can ever know how much and how sweetly and tenderly God loves them. Only with the help of his grace can we persevere in spiritual contemplation with endless wonder at his high, surpassing, immeasurable love which, in his goodness, He has for us.[23]

These are tough times in our world today, no matter where you live. Wars rage. Economies are in trouble. We are challenged by changes to our climate and shortages of food and water. In the aftermath of Covid, things have been tough on the road to recovery in many places. Some have yet to even begin that journey. But Julian says:

He [Jesus] did not say, 'You will never have a rough passage, you will never be over-strained, you will never feel uncomfortable,' but he did say, 'You will never be overcome'.[24]

The greatest commandment is written down. It is also spoken. You may hear it too. But unless you show it, then you have not heard it or understood it. To learn it and know it is to show it. Love is God's sign language. Learn the language God speaks in. The only language that God would wish you to be fluent in. Not English. Not Cantonese. The language of love.

This is God's kingdom currency. It is the cost God pays out in Christ – endlessly. God's love currency flows forever. The Christian life is dedicated to building God's kingdom and not preserving the church at all costs. What is needed in our churches today is a spiritual, political and economic reset that is aligned with kingdom values rather than 'churchy' concerns. God came among us in poverty and need, to tell us that in serving the poor, we will show our love for him. As one poet wrote: 'God's residence is next to mine, his furniture is love.'[25]

This is the universal language of faith, humanity and hope. It is the only language that will ever make peace and heal the hurts and trauma of nations and peoples at war. God's love holds us through all grief, anger or loss. Love is the greatest.

So, when we remember Christ moving from the sign of love in foot-washing to the sign of love on the cross, let me leave you with some words written by Julian almost a thousand years ago about what this sign represents:

> Would you learn your Lord's meaning in this thing? Learn it well: Love was His meaning. Who showed it you? Love. What did He show you? Love. Why did He show this? For Love. Hold this inside yourself, and you will learn and know more of the same. But you shall never know nor learn other things without this. So, I learned that Love was our Lord's meaning. Love.[26]

10

Thirty pieces of silver

Then one of the twelve, whose name was Judas Iscariot, went to the chief priests and said, 'What will you give me if I deliver him over to you?' And they paid him thirty pieces of silver. And from that moment he sought an opportunity to betray [Jesus].

MATTHEW 26:14–16

Judas stained-glass window at St Nicholas' Church, Moreton, Dorset.

The charity Samaritans was founded in 1953 by the Revd Chad Varah, at the time a young curate in the city (and diocese) of Lincoln. It is no exaggeration to say that the organisation, which is now international, and counsels the lonely, depressed and suicidal, grew out of a particular encounter that Varah had with shame and remorse. Cycling back to his clergy lodgings one day, he was greeted by the housekeeper at the door, who told him that his rector was ill, so he would need, at the last minute, to take a funeral. He cycled off to the cemetery, cassock flapping in the breeze.

When Varah arrived at the cemetery, the funeral was about to start. At this point, he did not know the name of the deceased but was curious about why the body was laid to rest in an unmarked plot and in the part of the cemetery that was not consecrated for burial. He finished the funeral but then began to ask some questions. Varah ascertained that he had just presided over the funeral of a girl of 13 who had killed herself because she had begun menstruating. Mortified that the girl had to be buried in unconsecrated ground, with parts of the burial liturgy redacted as it was a suicide, Varah felt his own remorse. The family were there too – and no less remorseful. Shame and guilt lay thick in the air, held together with the collective remorse of the mourners.

Varah's response to his remorse, and the guilt and shame of the mourners, was constructive and imaginative. He became concerned about the state of sex education for teenagers in the city and started to work with young people, especially listening to those who were contemplating suicide. Varah's Samaritans movement grew rapidly when he subsequently moved to London. Within ten years, Samaritans was a sizable charity, offering a supportive and empathetic listening service that was not political or religious.

I wrote this chapter during a week when I learned that an old school friend had taken his own life. His father, brother and a brother-in-law were all clergy. The deceased was married, with grown-up children. This was a clergy family through-and-through, deeply embedded in faith and love and shaped by the hope and grace of the gospel.

Despair can strike anyone. My old school friend took his life after a prolonged period struggling with depression. The cycle of depression and despair sucked him ever-downwards. But only, I think, and ultimately, into the everlasting arms of God. The days when mourners were left with the remorse and stigma of a family member who took their own life are, thankfully, mostly gone. We now speak differently of these deaths. For we understand the power of remorse to cause deep damage to individuals and to families, communities and nations. It is only in recent times that we have begun to understand quite why so many German citizens took their own lives as World War II ended.

For a few, it was their Nazi zeal and not wanting to live in a world without their Führer and where the Reich was decimated. For many, however, it was their own multiple overwhelming of shame and remorse that triggered taking their own life. The raped; the silent witnesses and bystanders, who had watched the trains trundling to the camps, and always leaving empty, but who had said nothing; those who had saved their own lives by betraying others. Indeed, many chose to symbolise that sense of being swamped by their individual and collective sins by drowning themselves and their children.[27]

Remorse is not an easy subject to dwell on, to be sure. But it is ironic that it should be so neglected in our world today, when shame, vilification and regret are so amplified in our social media – and often with such tragic consequences. As one recent celebrity pleaded before taking their own life, in their final social media post to their many followers: 'In a world where you can be anything, be kind.'

The scriptures are full of remorseful characters, and they pepper the Old and New Testaments with their biographies. Lives lived out of regret are painful to engage with, and the scriptures give us plenty of insight into this, yet as part of the overall ecology of salvation. Without question, the primary case study in remorse is Judas. In Christian tradition the name of Judas is synonymous with betrayal and possession. In Dante's *Inferno* Judas belongs in the inner ring of hell along with Cassius and Brutus, the other two arch-traitors.

And yet the New Testament tells us very little about Judas, who he was, why he betrayed Jesus and what on earth possessed him. That's why I have such a soft spot for this poem by Ruth Etchells, called 'The Ballad of the Judas Tree':

In Hell there grew a Judas Tree
Where Judas hanged and died
Because he could not bear to see
His master crucified.
Our Lord descended into Hell
And found his Judas there
For ever hanging on the tree
Grown from his own despair.
So Jesus cut his Judas down
And took him in his arms.
'It was for this I came,' he said,
'And not to do you harm.
My Father gave me twelve good men
And all of them I kept,
Though one betrayed and one denied,
Some fled and others slept.
In three days' time I must return
To make the others glad,
But first I had to come to Hell
And share the death you had.
My tree will grow in place of yours.
Its roots lie here as well.
There is no final victory
Without this soul from Hell.'
So when we all condemned him
As of every traitor worst,
Remember that, of all his men,
Our Lord forgave him first.

There is a very old tradition that Judas was the nephew of Caiaphas the high priest and persuaded to become a secret agent to plot the downfall of Jesus. In John's gospel we are told that Judas betrayed Jesus for the money (John 12:6) and that Judas was a thief. In the other gospels the name Iscariot seems to be linked to a fanatical set of Jewish nationalists who were determined to overthrow their Roman masters. According to this tradition of possession, Judas is gripped by zealotism, and when he realises that Jesus is not going to be the new political Messiah he had hoped for, he hands him over for betrayal. As one modern poet says ('Judas Restored', by Ann Lewin):

> My road to hell was paved
> With good intentions:
> I thought he'd fight, and show them
> He was king.
> But I was wrong.
> I couldn't live, knowing I had
> Betrayed the one I loved. I thought
> I'd have to bear that guilt for ever.
> But I was wrong again.
> No Sabbath rest for him:
> He came in awesome power,
> Trampled the gates of hell
> And conquered Death, taking
> All who were trapped in darkness
> To live with him in everlasting light.
> Purged by another kiss
> He's set me free
> To love him to eternity.[28]

We also read in John 13:27 and Luke 22:3 that Judas was possessed by Satan – 'Satan entered into him' – giving us the idea that Judas is somehow taken over by the devil in order to accomplish the wickedest of deeds. One modern writer suggests that Jesus is 'betrayed somewhere in the lost childhood of Judas'. It wasn't his fault – blame his parents.

Whether Judas was in it for the money, was politically disaffected, or was possessed by the devil, all the gospel writers seem to agree that he is sick and evil. Of course, these three potential motives are not in themselves competitive theories about Judas' betrayal; they may in fact turn out to be complementary.

The point is that when a gross and evil act is committed, even the gospel writers are not above the language of blame and scapegoating. In shifting the responsibility – all too easily from a tragic and suicidal human individual on to an evil and cosmic dimension, in which Satan appears to triumph over God – they miss a trick.

Judas is part of a problematic economy in the gospels: those who are vilified by the evangelists. Even gospels of salvation name their enemies, and this problem, ironically, reaches its peak in Holy Week. It begins in churches all over the land on Palm Sunday, with the dramatic reading of the Passion narratives. Congregations are reminded that it was the Jews who called for Jesus to be crucified: 'His blood be on us and on our children!' (Matthew 27:25). The readings leave us in no doubt that the blame for Jesus' death comes partly from a Jewish crowd, baying for blood. Judas is at the end of this narrative, the arch-betrayer and instrument of Satan. Greed and disenchantment get the better of him. The Romans, strangely, are just Gentiles going about their job; Jesus' execution isn't their fault.

The anti-Semitic tone of some of the Passion narratives make many Christians squirm today. This is part of our remorse for the Holocaust, and for which we bear our share of responsibility. Likewise, the treatment of Judas at the hands of the gospel writers is painful to read today. Placing blame on one race or one man seems crude, simplistic and even primitive. Is not abrogation just as much of a betrayal?

Yet our society has not evolved as much as one might hope. Those crude instincts reflected in the gospels live on today, as any failed national sports hero or politician can bear witness. One person to blame is convenient and neat; it lets us off the hook.

Judas is, in reality, a mirror to Jesus. He too can cry: 'Forgive them, for they know not what they do.' He is despised and rejected, a man acquainted with grief. He gets mixed up in the politics and passion of the week and kills himself in despair. He dies with no hope or security; like Jesus, he has been misunderstood, his mission has failed. This sentiment is captured in Peter De Rosa's poem, 'Judas'.

Judas, of course, is not the only betrayer in Holy Week. Consider Peter, who now realises that there is nowhere to hide and no one else to go to. So, he leaves the threatening light of the fire in the high priest's house, and goes out, not into the darkness of Judas' damnation, but into darkness of the night – where Christ is already to be found.

Dorothy Sayers' poem 'The Gates of Paradise' captures the encounter with Christ in the darkness of hell's most powerful night. The poem tells of the journey that Judas makes in the hours immediately after his death, across a lonely desert. He meets the two thieves who died with Christ. But when they learn who he is and of what he is guilty, they refuse to accompany him. Eventually Judas encounters a grey-hooded man who agrees to walk with him to the gates of Hell and beyond.

Many years ago, the artist Sir Laurence Whistler created a set of 13 engraved glass windows for a church, consisting of twelve disciples, with the 13th being for Christ. It was the twelfth of these windows featuring Judas (see the photo on p. 125) that was the subject of much controversy, because the parish rejected it. (The parish church in Moreton, Dorset, did eventually accept and install the window almost 30 years later, in 2014.) What might have caused the church to reject the window? It might have been the disturbing image of a man committing suicide, or perhaps that some in the parish felt Judas did belong in hell, with Cassius and Brutus.

But Whistler drew on other Christian traditions. Julian of Norwich, for example, who in one of her showings went to hell and found no one there, 'not even a Jew'. Catherine of Sienna said she could not go to heaven if there was anyone in hell. Whistler's window was nicknamed 'the forgiveness window', and it has Judas with a rope around his neck being pulled into heaven. As he is, the coins (blood money) fall from his hands and become petals and blossoming flowers on the ground.

This is the very inversion of Dante's vision of what befell Judas, and, of course, it ties in with another rather nice modern myth about Judas. Noting that on Good Friday and after the death of Jesus, all the disciples dispersed and ran away, one modern poet, Norma Farber ('Compassion') asks where we might find Mary, the mother of Jesus on that day? Perhaps she is comforting Judas' mother.

An ecology of kindness and grace is part of the deep core rubble that forms the foundations of God's love. Judas' remorse is an extreme mirror of what could befall any of us. We all make mistakes. We all have regrets. We can all be imprisoned by remorse. We can then, all too easily, travel the road to deeper despair, instead of being drawn into the route and home of abiding, abundant love. Understanding remorse, but knowing we can't let it shape the rest of our lives, is what allows the prodigal son to take one step back towards home.

So, to the despised and rejected, God says, through Christ, that he too will know something of that rejection. The scripting and patterning of this in the life of Jesus is as important for the story of salvation as is the cross. You have to see it as a whole. Sometimes the rejection is active, and sometimes quite passive, but Jesus is sensate to both. This is integral to God's incarnation: the Word became flesh. God knows precisely what it is to be human. Jesus is, after all, the body language of God. Jesus enacts what God would do with our shame and remorse. So, Jesus touches the untouchable; sees the unseen; hears the unheard; speaks for and to the unspoken; embraces the excluded. This includes inculcating our own deepest pains, which are often not only imprinted on the body, but also in the soul and heart.

To understand Judas properly within the context of God's economy, we must appreciate something obvious but seldom stated enough: God's love is complete, total, free, overwhelming – so much so, that it is, in human terms, irrational. The currency of God's kingdom flows, and it is abundant and buoyant. God is to be praised, not to be appeased, because God loves us totally and enjoys us as we are, remorse and all.

Dan Hardy, a friend of mine and a very fine theologian too, used to say that the biggest problem facing the church throughout history, now in the present, and in the future to come, is always, ever, the same: coping with the overwhelming abundance and love of God. My friend said that the churches never really understood it, and constantly struggled with the immeasurable grace, love and mercy of God. The church wants to direct this love and ideally ration it out to the (apparently) more deserving.

But the life of Jesus embodies the body language of God. Love for all – especially those on the margins and those crippled with guilt and remorse. Partly for this reason, I find the modern poem 'Praise', by Harry Smart, particularly compelling.

There is a (likely) apocryphal tale of a competition to write a very short sermon for radio. The winner was reputedly called 'The Kiss', and it went like this: 'Good to have you home, son. Sorry you were in so much pain.' 'It wasn't the nails that hurt, dad. It was the kiss.'

Our attention is drawn to the deeply physical act of kissing: the kissing of Jesus' feet by an unknown woman; the kiss of Judas in betrayal. But whatever kind of kiss it was, the point is simple. God dwelt with us, among us and as one of us: the Word made flesh. And it is that flesh that returns to heaven in the ascension. Even flesh marked by pain, torment and torture.

The flesh that Jesus returns to heaven with is even more like ours: it has been loved and cherished, but also weathered, beaten, rejected, despised and defeated. Finally, it has died. This is the flesh of the resurrection too. The one still marked with nails, but now raised.

11

Gambling at the foot of the cross

> For since, in the wisdom of God, the world did not know God through wisdom, it pleased God through the folly of what we preach to save those who believe. For Jews demand signs and Greeks seek wisdom, but we preach Christ crucified, a stumbling block to Jews and folly to Gentiles, but to those who are called, both Jews and Greeks, Christ the power of God and the wisdom of God. For the foolishness of God is wiser than men, and the weakness of God is stronger than men.
>
> 1 CORINTHIANS 1:21–25

In C.S. Lewis' *The Lion, the Witch and Wardrobe*, the mocking of Aslan is perhaps the most distressing and moving scene in the whole book. It is here, perhaps, rather than at the actual point of death, that we really begin to encounter the weakness of Aslan, the hero-lion of the allegory. To save the three children from the forces of darkness, Aslan surrenders himself. Like Jesus allowing himself to be handed over to injustice and certain death, Aslan gives himself up – his life and strength – to mockery, torture and cruel execution. Aslan becomes too weak and passive to resist the taunts of the creatures that circle around their captive.

The cross of Christ dislocates, dismantles and ultimately destroys the monopoly that had been imposed on monotheism. The death of Jesus is the end of religious tribalism as a means of salvation. Purification rites, rituals, expensive sacrifices, hierarchy and obeisance – all of which cost money to those who had the means to procure participation in the life of faith – are terminated at the cross. Citizenship is now free to all who seek it. The wages of sin might well have been death, but you can no longer buy yourself out of debt. It has been paid in full.

In Christ, there is neither Jew or Greek, slave or free, male or female, barren or fecund. In this, such is the love of God that – even to flawed vessels like us, with our mistranslations, missteps and mistakes – Jesus comes bearing the offer of mercy, grace and love. He offers it to strangers, aliens and foreigners; to the diseased, the disfigured and the demonised; to orphans and widows; to prostitutes and sinners; to the stigmatised and the marginalised. God is *for* us all. The old tribalism is now subverted by multicultural regionalism (i.e. Israel, but also Samaria, Idumea, Gerasene, etc.) to become a true eventual internationalism and globalisation.

Furthermore, the New Testament presents us with some pressing questions about the church's attempts to police its borders and apply moral, social or other forms of tax and levy on those who wish to be included. The nature–nurture axis is what produces our normativity in relation to sexuality and, equally, what societies come to regard as taboo or deviant.

The New Testament is flush with examples of people who are quite powerless to alter what they are, and they may find themselves on the wrong end of social, moral, temporal and cultural projections that label them as deviants. They lack the agency to change what they are or have been made to become. It matters not whether they were born this way or that or have been made this way by their circumstances or upbringing. They must be loved as they are. Thus, the saying 'We hate the sin, but not the sinner' is all very well, but we don't find such neat distinctions in the gospels.

Paul counselled slaves that they may not be able to change their day-to-day drudgery and the demands made upon them, and simply must continue being good, reliable and obedient workers, even as Christians. That meant they would still have no actual human right to refuse the demands of their owners, and that those would have frequently included sexual ultimatums, abuse, violations and violence. With the recent recovery of African American history and in liberation, ethnic, feminist, political and other theologies of resistance and revolution, Christians have had to come to terms with their collusion in privileging white male normativity.

The targeting, sexual abuse, deliberate humiliation and physical emasculation of black men in early-to-mid 20th century America, then with tarring and feathering often preceding their eventual castration before the lynching, and all set as a spectacle before the prurient curiosity of large gatherings of white crowds, is well chronicled. You could even buy souvenir postcards of such events.

I think of the words uttered before Jesus in the court of Caiaphas: 'What further witnesses do we need?' (Matthew 26:65). Just as black men were dragged from the county jail and lynched before trial or verdict, so it is with Jesus – condemned to death before the defence or prosecution has presented their case. I mean, why bother with the due process of justice or the courts? We know who the guilty are and what the consequences shall be. Let us take this to the final stage and save money and time.

So, we come to the crucifixion. And here, you might find the next few paragraphs rather difficult. I think we must learn to see in Jesus someone who is a victim of abuse, and by this, I include sexual abuse, taunting, shaming and humiliation. We know that Jesus was stripped, whipped, scourged and mocked. You may find his silence eloquent, powerful or puzzling. I think in our age, his silence echoes and cries across two thousand years of sexual, marital, emotional and physical abuse. The #MeToo and #ChurchToo movements teach us that victims have been pressed and pushed into silence. Their voices and cries are not heard, and the bystanders – the many – do nothing to rein in the cruelty of the few.

Jesus was whipped in a way that flayed his skin, the thorn crown was forced on to his head to humiliate and to hurt. The timing of events, an all-night trial so that he was exhausted, the walk with the cross up the hill in the hottest part of the day, encouraging the sweat of his body to increase the pain of the broken skin, the rough wood of the cross, the nails, the exposure, the thirst, the slow painful suffocation – all of this torture aimed to maximise the physical pain which he had to bear.

The two others crucified alongside him also had to suffer this cruel torture; whatever their guilt, it is unlikely that they 'deserved' to die in such agony. The soldiers had learnt to do their job, nail them up, eventually break their legs and pass the time with a bit of gambling while waiting for the agony to end. We forget that the groups of men hitting, striking, beating, spitting at and abusing Jesus blindfolded him and taunted him. They kept their deeds in the dark. There would be no witnesses.

This was all part of the shame culture invested in humiliating prisoners and the condemned. They were now sub-human and would shortly be extinguished forever. The silence of the victims might have been stoicism or possibly bravery. More likely, however, it is utter terror and paralysing fear.

As we now know from firsthand accounts of crucifixions two thousand years ago, the victim might be forced to watch their family or friends brutalised, sodomised, beaten or raped while they, the powerless, were compelled to watch. The privilege of the state was the power of terror. Further shaming, mutilation and offences could be committed against a person who was pinned and tied to a cross.

Shame culture was the deliberate stripping of a man's dignity and honour. Victims of crucifixion were often pinned up naked, with their slow death through asphyxiation producing their own perverse offshoot: the sexual spectacle of a man writhing, gasping for breath, while every soft organ and muscle swelled bulbous purple with blood.

Crucifixion-induced shame rendered the victim unable to exercise any self-control of their muscles, motions or reflexes in their body, and the sadistic cruelty this involved added to the public humiliation. Perhaps you can now understand why the disciples had very good reasons to be scarce at the foot of the cross. Getting caught up in a crucifixion – as the friend or family of the victim – could be dangerous for witnesses. Or they might just be forced to watch the violent and degrading impalement of a victim's orifices while still alive.

So maybe now you can understand why the soldiers laughed at the foot of the cross, and gamed with dice, banter, torments and insults, while casually inflicting just a little bit more pain. The violation of each victim was a crucial component in their subjugation and eventual extinction. We, too, are crucified with Christ. Yes, #WeToo.

The cross is a specimen sample of our cruelty and inhumanity. Crucifixion was a carefully choreographed and planned process of execution. Just like other forms of torture, it was not designed to be quick. Just like other forms of public execution, it was designed to gratify, terrify, pacify and horrify the witnesses. As a public spectacle, it was an expedient means to eliminate criminals, troublemakers, deviants and rebels. The whole exhibition and display of this crucifixion in Jerusalem represents a tense trade-off and collusion between the religious status quo and an oppressive regime.

Good Friday should not minimise or sanitise the physical horror of Christ's crucifixion. Yet what it represents is the reality of torture and death deliberately perpetrated. The sufferings of Good Friday are part of the ecology of pain. But crucifixion is not the kind of pain that might lead to new birth or some sweaty achievement. This pain has nothing to do with the 'sweet' pains of labour or the sweat and toil of a hard day's work.

No, this is pain inflicted only to taunt, harm and destroy. Deliberately designed to be brutal and cruel, it is consciously meted out. This is the kind of pain inflicted by sadists, bullies or self-serving oppressive regimes. To perpetrate such torture, you either need to switch off or be turned on by it.

Jesus' closest witnesses are terrified by it and make themselves scarce. Only a few followers remain at the foot of the cross to keep vigil. Jesus accepts this suffering, enduring the cross without reproach. Some came hoping for a spectacle. Perhaps a few come hoping for a miracle. Some come to mock. Others come to gamble and take bets on how long the victims will last.

Others gain a form of pleasure or ghoulish frisson from watching another suffer. Perhaps it boosts their sense of self-righteousness. Then there is a perverse pleasure in watching the mighty fall, or someone once adored and popular by the people now left with no supporters or friends. We love a rags-to-riches story, but we take a secret pleasure in a riches-to-rags sequel. We put the chosen few on a pedestal or podium. We also reserve the right to take them down or knock them off it and then trample them underfoot.

The crucifixion requires a budget, too. The soldiers must be paid, and the instruments of death purchased. Trials, even rigged ones, cost money. The cost of Christian living begins with an unjust death. Remember, then, that injustice needs a budget, accountant, income and audit.

Some at the cross are just doing their job, just as the Roman soldiers are. They are the mere instruments for actions that were determined by earlier court proceedings. Meanwhile, somebody carved the wood for the cross, and somebody made the ropes and the nails. Marshalls for the crowds are there. There must be a report of the death, so there is a notetaker. Somebody has to do the work, and it is only fair that those who do become hardened to their role and tasks.

It seems reasonable, doesn't it, that those employed to do their job that Friday afternoon do so in a way that must de-personalise the convicted? In the eyes of the law, they have already been dehuman-ised, literally. Once the sentence was passed, the convicted ceased to exist as persons. Those on duty that day do what is normal for routine executions. They play dice for the clothing of the condemned, perhaps as a trophy or souvenir. Or maybe Jesus' cloak was worth wearing and could be sold on? We'll never know. So, the soldiers laugh and joke, and also gamble for what is worth saving – Jesus' cloak.[29]

Where does this leave us with the cross? In life, death is unavoidable. In living and loving, pain is also unavoidable. But what is the actual currency of pain in the crucifixion? What is being transacted here? What is spent and bought, lost and gained? Pain is an integral part of the human condition. Yet, what we are exposed to here is the creation of pain. This is pain being used to control others. This pain is meant to induce fear, shame, degrade, torment, humiliate and break its victims.

On the cross, Jesus took our greatest fears, pain, alienation and death into the aching heart of God. To the world, this looks like nothing other than foolishness, because Christians proclaim that God experienced not just the horror of the cross but also the reality of death. This is the scandalous suggestion that Paul calls a 'stumbling block' to Jews and foolishness to Greeks (i.e. Gentiles). After all, how can the creator of all that is, the Almighty, Eternal Being, experience the mortal finality of death? It makes no sense.

The gospels show us that Jesus, who started out with many friends and followers, is now deserted. Alone, he hangs there, with just his accusers, some criminals and casual bystanders for company. He saved others, but he cannot save himself. Yet, in the reality of the cross, we find God fully experiencing the abandonment of death and the deepest anguish and suffering we can know. The loss of our most beloved. Christ, who is crucified, is foolishness to the world. But to us, this is the power of God made perfect in total weakness (unto death) and utter annihilation. In this lies the promise of salvation.

Themes of darkness and light once again return to the gospels as they record the last gasps of Jesus. The shadows and flames of the previous night, in which Peter lurked, are now dominated by a 'darkness over the whole land' (Mark 15:33). It is the afternoon, however, so this darkness, both literally and metaphorically, seems to be the gospels' way of acknowledging the whole of creation's bereavement at this point.

Good Friday is the axis point of abandonment. Jesus is not being saved. He is dying. He is not saved. He is dead. The loud cry and the last breath cue the temple curtain to be torn in two, as though in this death, paradoxically, all division between humanity and divinity is now finally ripped apart.

This is why one witness – the centurion – is given the ultimate words of testimony at this point in the narrative: truly, this person was God's Son. Yet just as our focus comes to a single point on a single hill, each of the gospel writers skilfully directs our gaze to some unremarkable figures in the background who have witnessed the torture and execution.

Mary, Mary Magdalene, Salome and others – the few who have followed Jesus – are companions to the end. We cannot know what risks they took to be there. But their witnessing of these events will have important consequences for what happens next. It is to these women that the task of recognising Jesus in the light of Easter will now fall. Those who saw him die will be the first to see him alive.

The English Christian mystic Margery Kempe (1373–1438) claimed God once said to her, 'More pleasing to me than all your prayers, works and penances is that you would believe I love you.' Christ died for all (John 1:12; 3:16). Paul, writing to Titus put it better than any theologian:

> But when the goodness and loving kindness of God our Saviour appeared, he saved us, not because of works done by us in righteousness, but according to his own mercy, by the washing of regeneration and renewal of the Holy Spirit, whom he poured out on us richly through Jesus Christ our Saviour, so that being justified by his grace we might become heirs according to the hope of eternal life.
> TITUS 3:4–7

Jesus could not save himself, and we cannot save ourselves. The kindness and love of God are nonetheless offered and free. No sanctions are imposed. Salvation is not something we eventually acquire, provided we are very, very good. We are invited to throw ourselves on God's mercy, accept Christ as our redeemer and rejoice. We have all sinned. We all fall short of God's glory. No one deserves heaven.

The gospel simply boils down to this. Accept Jesus and welcome him into your life and habitat, and God will share his life and home with you for eternity. Yet far too many Christians profess belief in the unmerited grace of God but behave as though salvation can be earned if they try harder. But the church is not meant to be modelling some kind of business that runs a loyalty reward-card scheme: the more you attend or buy, the better the perks are for the members. The church is a field hospital for the wounded and broken, the sinner and the despairing, and those beyond hope. It is for all of us.

In all this, we must remember that God's love is broader and deeper than anything we can conceive. God's love is not rationed. In fact, it is so comprehensive as to be almost irrational. We offer a church for all, because God's kingdom is for all. The scriptures are so beautifully frank: 'God is love, and whoever abides in love abides in God, and God abides in him' (1 John 4:16). You cannot buy love. It is costly, yet free. Such is the currency of the kingdom of God.

12

Burial costs

> After these things Joseph of Arimathea, who was a disciple
> of Jesus, but secretly for fear of the Jews, asked Pilate that
> he might take away the body of Jesus, and Pilate gave him
> permission. So he came and took away his body. Nicodemus
> also, who earlier had come to Jesus by night, came bringing
> a mixture of myrrh and aloes, about seventy-five pounds in
> weight. So they took the body of Jesus and bound it in linen
> cloths with the spices, as is the burial custom of the Jews. Now
> in the place where he was crucified there was a garden, and in
> the garden a new tomb in which no one had yet been laid. So
> because of the Jewish day of Preparation, since the tomb was
> close at hand, they laid Jesus there.
> JOHN 19:38–42

Although Jesus is now dead, the gospels carefully note that Pilate is
surprised (Mark 15:44). There is almost an implication of nonchalance
on the part of Pilate as Joseph of Arimathea petitions him for the body
of Jesus. One can imagine Pilate distancing himself from the day's
events with casual small talk: 'Is he dead already? Really? Someone
go and check, will they? Ah, it seems he is – well, I never. They usually
last a bit longer on the cross… Ah well, yes, I suppose you can have
the body. I mean, why not?'

After the trials, tribulations and trauma of Jesus' death, we suddenly
find ourselves immersed in a surprising sense of solace and com-
posure. If you have ever sat with family or friends at the actual point of
a loved one's death, there is often a sense of passing and peace before

the grief begins to be realised. Pilate is not upset, of course. He's not really bothered at all.

Pilate's unsettling indifference is juxtaposed with the detailed account of Jesus' burial, starkly contrasting the rapid narration of his demise. We are informed about the tomb's owner, the linen cloth for Jesus' wrapping and the meticulous arrangements for the burial and sealing of the grave. The gospels painstakingly emphasise that the burial of Jesus was executed with utmost care and attention to detail, evoking a profound sense of reverence and respect.

The cost of burial is carefully laid out: a tomb, spices, ointment, myrrh and aloes. John's gospel mentions Nicodemus and Joseph of Arimathea as paying meticulous care to the preparation of Jesus' body – the wrapping in strips of linen and a burial cloth. Though the burial is hurried, it has cost money, time and courage to still see it is done properly.

Now we find ourselves in the realm of the undertakers. Jesus' earthly journey has concluded, and the gospels provide the expected details: the place and manner of his burial and, perhaps, how to commemorate him. A visit to the shrine, maybe? However, this is not the conclusion the gospels draw. Death, it seems, is not the final chapter. It is merely the beginning, a twist that leaves us intrigued and curious.

In the Eastern Church, the women who walk to the tomb on the first Sunday of Easter are also known as the Myrrhbearers. These women rise early and make their way to the tomb carrying the oils to tend to the body. There are burial costs to attend to. Joseph of Arimathea has kindly given Jesus' body a place in a newly hewn tomb he paid for. Jesus is wrapped in a shroud, too, which has also been gifted.

The women come with their expensive oils, ointments, spices and herbs to anoint and cherish this tortured corpse. Traditionally, there are eight women – Mary Magdalene, Joanna, Susanna, Salome, Mary the wife of Cleopas, Mary and Martha of Bethany, and Mary the mother of Jesus. The first five are named in the gospels as some women who came from Galilee with Jesus. Mary, Martha and Mary the mother of Jesus are traditionally included among the Myrrhbearers, even though the gospels do not mention them as part of the early morning group.

We know that the women had watched from a distance at the crucifixion. There was nothing they could do to change the situation, but their presence as witnesses to these tragic events is crucial. They stood firm and, in doing so, stood with mothers, wives and daughters over the centuries who have witnessed and watched as their loved ones were tortured and killed through the cruelty and brutality of oppressive regimes.

They followed, we are told, to where the tomb was located and noted its position. Then they had to wait. Nothing could interrupt the sabbath. So, grieving and broken, they kept the sabbath rituals and the day of rest. Once the sabbath was over, they could act. They could do nothing to cancel the horror of Good Friday. But here now, there is one expensive, costly act of love they can perform with the body of their beloved Jesus. The precious oils, herbs and spices were gathered, and the women's party set off. They went to the tomb just as the sun rose upon the garden.

In some respects, this was rather naïve. The women knew the tomb had been sealed with a stone, and they had not thought through how this was to be moved. Perhaps as a group, they could? They speak of the impracticalities, but it does not stop their journey. They are driven by the need to show commitment and love, even though the one they love is dead. To treat his body with honour and to do what they can is all they have left.

As the sun rises, they find that the stone has been rolled back, the grave is open, and an angel greets them with the standard angelic greeting: 'Do not be afraid' (Matthew 28:5). This is what the archangel Gabriel told Mary when announcing to her she was now with a child, carrying God's chosen. Just as the incarnation requires gestation, so does the resurrection.

The women are told that the crucified one is not here because he is alive. They are told to go and tell the disciples. Then Mary Magdalene and Mary encounter the risen Christ, and Jesus also reiterates that they are not to be afraid but to go and tell the others. The faithful vigil of the women, the love that took them to serve the body beyond its life, is rewarded with the first news of the resurrection, the first encounter with the risen Christ. Mary Magdalene, in the Orthodox tradition, is therefore the apostle to the apostles.

The cost–benefit axis is all too apparent. The women left their homes in darkness, and now they return in the light. They left in grief and return with a heady emotional mix of barely believable joy tempered with fear and incomprehension. They left in despair and mourning yet now return with a glimpse of hope and purpose. Yet the news they bring is so impossible, beyond any imagining, so contrary to logic, so far from the world's wisdom, that they are afraid.

They are right to fear that they will be dubbed irrational fantasists or emotional and hysterical women who have lost touch with reality. Unsurprisingly, the gospels record that their news is dismissed as an 'idle tale' typical of women. Then, as now, empirical rationality finds the resurrection impossible, and our faith nothing more than wishful thinking.

Yet faith has room for the God who can do the impossible, who has overcome death, sin and evil, and who has revealed the depths of love for each of us. Our faith knows that we are never alone, that though we may fall, we will never be destroyed, and that though we may falter, we are journeying to the promised land.

In Christ, there is no longer 'social distance' between us and God. God chose to dwell with us in Christ so that we might be one with another and one with God.

Bringing about the kingdom of God is, therefore, what Christian faith is about. It is not supposed to be the church preservation society (good work though such bodies undoubtedly do for our heritage and spirituality). Christianity is a faith of touch and bonding. If you don't believe me, just look at the number of people Jesus touches in the gospels. Jesus is the body language of God. He sees the unseen, hears the unheard and touches the untouchable. The incarnation closes the gap between humanity and divinity.

The events of Easter, just like Christmas, affirm that the world, as we know it, has been turned upside down. Life has come into the world. Death has no more dominion. The incarnation represents new life. The resurrection represents new life. Both Easter and Christmas state that the old order is passing away. And behold, a new order is being born.

That is what Christians first believed, and they had every reason to: they experienced the confounding of their old common life. Instead of cherishing the memory of a dead charismatic Galilean preacher and healer, they were faced with something wholly other: a resurrection commanding and creating a new social and moral order. This is Christianity: not simply a personal relationship with Jesus, but a commitment to living our communal life utterly differently from what went before.

From the very beginning, Christianity was a tactile – yes, a touching – faith. This new religious movement looked after widows and orphans. It gathered to break bread. It was congregational and social. It redistributed wealth and gave alms.

In the meantime, we are on our own road to Emmaus. Just as the two unnamed disciples found (Luke 24:13–35), Jesus' resurrection *re-minds* us. The resurrection changes the way we think, act and feel. Easter constantly calls us back to the core of our faith. We are bonded together to *re-mind* the world that resurrection changes our moral and social order. Knitted together in acts of charity, love, service and sacrifice, we discover the touching places between our humanity and divinity, solitude and society. Standing amid this is the resurrected Christ – the sign of God's abundant love and grace that we are bidden to offer to all.

There is a wonderful rawness to the resurrection stories. There are no 'I knew you'd be back' salutations from the more optimistic among the disciples. Rather, the gospel accounts of the resurrection convey fear, confusion, doubt and trepidation – all perfectly proper human reactions to seeing a dead man walking, talking and even eating a piece of broiled fish.

Thank goodness, then, that none of the four gospels end by giving us abstract doctrinal reflections in some kind of attempt to explain the resurrection. It cannot be. It is a matter of faith, which is why the stories, for all their raggedness, fear, passion and breathless wonder, are the best vehicles Christians have for trying to narrate the first Easter. They give us Mary, weeping at the tomb, talking to someone who could be a gardener. And they give us the disciples, doubting what is plainly before their very eyes.

The advantage of stories is that they give us a deeper knowledge that abstract reasoning can never provide. Another advantage of 'story knowledge' is its particularity and exactness. Stories give us real people or characters in specific times and places who are doing actual things: coming to the tomb to lay flowers and anoint a body; running away scared when the grave is found to be empty; not recognising the gardener; walking with acquaintances on the road to Emmaus; not recognising the stranger you are breaking bread with.

One of the reasons John's accounts of the resurrection are so persuasive is that they effectively side with the doubters and leave the reader with lingering hesitancy. Indeed, it is only when Jesus begins to explain how the past has been fulfilled in the present – and how the present has now fulfilled the past – that we begin to gain a sense of how 'Peace be with you' might be more than a mere greeting.

Resurrections challenge our world views. They remind us that Jesus, in the light of Easter, puts all our religion in the shade. The task of the disciples is not to guard an empty tomb; it is to follow the risen Jesus and to try to understand how he appears to us afresh, even at the meal table. Easter is about finding and encountering the risen Jesus in the very present. 'Peace be with you' is not just a state of mind; it is part of the very core of being for the church.

So, a story of stark absence – Good Friday – is now one of intense presence. The reality of Jesus is now bigger than reality itself. And Jesus is no longer a figure of the past. Nor does he merely live through the memories of the disciples. When Jesus tells Mary Magdalene, 'Do not cling to me', and the disciples, 'Touch me', he is really saying something quite simple. You cannot hold on to the Jesus you once knew. You cannot have the past back. You cannot possess Jesus any longer. You can touch, but you cannot hold. But be assured, he will hold you.

Ultimately, the words of the gospels can never do justice to the reality of the resurrection. The first Easter is, simply, more than tongues can tell. However, the stories we are left with contain vital clues as to what to expect or hope for the future church. For example, John's account of the 153 variety of fish hauled up in the nets is probably trying to tell us something quite important about the future diversity of the church. The church will be as abundant as a fisherman's haul: full of interesting specimens.

John, in his recounting of the breakfast, is also saying something about hospitality: Jesus still invites us to feast with him. Even though the disciples deserted Jesus after the last supper, there were other suppers. Jesus is, in every sense, the host. We continue to feed on him and feed with him.

After the breakfast on the beach, Jesus continues teaching about provision. It is a threefold, almost maternal kind of caring and feeding that Jesus is advocating: feed my lambs; tend my sheep; feed my sheep. The invitation is to take an active lead in caring for, nourishing and providing for the flock – old and young alike, both lambs and sheep. Just as Jesus has provided breakfast, so must the disciples provide for those with whom they have been entrusted.

Then there is the swimming. One of the strange things about the Bible is that there is no real example of successful swimming before the resurrection. Water symbolises the forces of chaos and overwhelm. But after Easter, it is different. Peter can take the plunge. The resurrection appearances invite the disciples to take risks. The church will be advanced by those who can learn to swim or even to try to walk on water.

There is a Venetian proverb: 'The critic stands on the shore, but the artist swims in the sea.' In our resurrection faith, we are invited to take the plunge – not because we are rash but because Christ now beckons us to join him in a new life of adventure and hope.

In the resurrection, God gives us the true hope that dares to change the world. We are called to feed our people, tend our people and love our people – just as we are fed, loved and tended by his hands. The world is hungry for Christ, and that is why we try to respond by feeding the world with the bread of heaven and with the justice of God.

The Easter stories are, therefore, ultimately about showing that the 'Jesus project', which had looked doomed in the ashes of Good Friday, is somehow born out of the incredible and indescribable experiences of Easter Sunday. To modify a Swedish proverb, good theology is 'poetry plus, not science minus'.

So, at every Easter, the church does what it has done since AD33 (circa). It faces death. It is no use clinging to the past. The Easter message is that while we must continue to live alongside the world's suffering, we are meant to understand and live by the revolutionary freedom of the resurrection. The bursting from the tomb is the end of 'organised religion'. It breaks that power with revolutionary faith, which smashed the grip and power of religion with something else.

This new faith chooses pain, living alongside it and in suffering solidarity, offering hope by being there but also working to transform unjust structures that perpetuate torment. Often, such victims are left alive on the cross and made to struggle continually. Sometimes, we lose them to death. We are witnesses and must tell our brothers and sisters what we have seen.

The resurrection breaks all frames of reference, bursting our perceptual boundaries and leaving the gospel writers with the huge task of trying to piece together shards of information that exceed any sense of reality. An appearance here, a disappearance there, a sighting then, but a vanishing now; one minute, you can touch Jesus; the next, he's like an apparition.

We should see Easter not so much as the feast that puts the broken back together but as the Feast of Total Transformation. It fundamentally offers us a sense of re-creation. And the Easter stories are a narrative of light, not just because the darkness of Good Friday is dispersed and destroyed by the shattering light of the resurrection, but also because Jesus is recognised as the new light. This new light is so dazzling that it cannot be comprehended.

So, this light returns us to the first light of creation. This is a new dawn. God's light now shines – a sign of the realm of heaven, where there is neither day nor night but one light of equal brightness. This is a light beyond the sun, moon and stars. The light of the resurrection is the light of a whole new creation, a revelation of radiance that can barely be worded. Easter is the festival of fire, light and dawn – a new age dawns the moment the stone is rolled away, and the Son of God bursts forth in a radiant splendour that is blinding yet also illuminating. In this light, we are all now transformed – in our awe, wonder and worship.

How shall we live in this light? One way of understanding our new place in the world is to grasp that the scriptures are bookended and pivot in gardens. The Christian scriptures begin in Genesis with the expulsion from the garden of Eden. The centre takes us not just to the garden of Gethsemane (abandonment and betrayal) but also to the

Easter garden of resurrection. The Christian scriptures end with flowing rivers in Revelation and leaves on trees for the healing of nations. One eternal light and no more darkness.

One might also say that the resurrection plants a seed in us each year and asks us to permit the Spirit to water it and produce the growth God seeks. St Basil says:

> A tree is known by its fruit; a person by their deeds. A good deed is never lost; those who sow courtesy reap friendship, and those who plant kindness gather love.

If we reap what we sow, the returns on the investment of love we make will be returned with interest. God's currency is love and kindness. So, don't hoard it, waste it, bury it or try to stash it away. Don't use it for yourself. You cannot be rich in love on your own.

The parables of the talents (Matthew 25:14–30) and the minas (Luke 19:11–27) are only superficially about money. In truth, they are really stories about taking a risk with something you did not own or earn yet was given to you to make something of and invest. The task is not to say alive, but rather to be buried with Christ. Yes, we have our burial costs too. According to Romans 6:4, we have been buried with Christ through baptism into death. When Christ died and was buried, it was on our behalf. We are thus buried with him. Our baptism buries us with Christ in that death, and we are joined to Christ in that burial too, because God saves us and raises us to new life. That life is what God gives you.

Like God's love, see what you can do with what God gave you. You have no debts. They were paid long ago. Follow the example of Christ you find through the life and work of Jesus. Take the risk. The cost of Christian living invites you to let the currency of God's kingdom flow through you.

Endings: Mutuality and building society

Some years ago, my wife Emma and I had a young undergraduate living with us for around a year. Her family are close friends of ours, and she came to stay during an unexpected family bereavement. It was a couple of weeks before Christmas, and we were shopping for provisions in the Covered Market in Oxford. 'So how many days is a typical life?' she suddenly piped up. We did the sums and worked out that if you live to just beyond 80 – a bit more than your biblically allotted 'threescore years and ten' (Psalm 90:10, KJV) – you'll hit the 30,000 mark.

But 30,000 sounded like a rather small number to me. 'How many days have I lived?' I asked. '20,000,' she replied. I mused on the remaining 10,000 left; and wondered to myself how two-thirds had already passed. 'What about you?' I asked. She paused. 'I have clocked up 7,000; so about another 23,000 to go,' she announced, aware of the passing of the day. 'Do you know,' she suddenly said, 'the first 2,000 of my 7,000 – I barely remember them.' It was a conversation that has stayed with me. It is a reminder of the finite nature of life, that time is precious.

The term 'building society' first arose in the late 18th century in Great Britain from cooperative savings groups. John and Charles Wesley, when they were undergraduates, founded a collection of small groups that promoted thrift, mutuality and holiness. These were often dubbed 'Holiness Clubs'. John and Charles Wesley formed Christ Church, Oxford's first club, in 1729. The religious progeny was Methodism – literally, a methodical way of going about one's faith. The more secular progeny found expression in cooperatives, and also what we now call building societies.

Think of the term for a moment. These societies arose in the heartlands of Methodism in the late 18th century. Some of these building societies were just about building society. A network of clubs and societies for cooperation and the exchange of ideas among highly active citizenry. Some were about enabling home-ownership.

Most of the original societies were fully *terminating*, where they would be dissolved when all members had a house: the last of them, the First Salisbury and District Perfect Thrift Building Society, was only wound up in March 1980. But in the 19th century, a new development took place with the establishment of the *permanent building society*, where the society continued on a rolling basis, continually taking in new members as earlier ones completed their own house purchases.

Today, the Nationwide is the world's biggest building society. In 1884, Alfred Idle was their first borrower, and was renting a house when he first moved to Battersea; but then the Southern Co-operative Permanent Building Society arranged a mortgage of £120. Much of the new social housing was berthed in neighbourhoods that were rooted in temperance and thrift and mutuality.

Mutuality, charity and a concern for economic justice marked out the very first Christian communities. Stephen, the first Christian martyr, was a deacon with special responsibility for the daily distribution of alms to widows and orphans (Acts 6:1–3), reflecting the commitment of the church to charity and service advocated in the gospels. In character, the first churches, although diverse in practice and belief, appear nevertheless to have exhibited a radical openness to mutuality, parity and inclusion. Indeed, and as we noted earlier, the term for 'church' is the simple Greek word *ekklesia*, meaning the 'assembly of the people' who belong to but are called out of their community. All over the Mediterranean world, assemblies determined the politics, polity and civic ordering of communities and cities. But they were usually only open to citizens, and the power to speak and vote was normally confined to men.

The assemblies of the New Testament church were, in contrast, inclusive bodies and models of mutuality. In these *ekklesia*, women were admitted, as were slaves (compare Paul's letter to Philemon), children, foreigners and other visitors. In other words, the character of the New Testament *ekklesia* represented and embodied a different kind of spiritual and social ordering that eschewed discrimination on grounds of race, gender and other criteria.

As with the word ecology (see chapter 3), the very term 'economics' is rooted in the Greek word *oikos* – the concept of a well-managed, stewarded household. *Oikos* was one of the early terms for 'church' – literally, the 'household of faith'. In terms of etymology, the management of the household was linked to the budget. It is no accident that Jesus told so many parables about stewardship and money, linked to the church.

So, implicit in the term *oikos* is not merely an idea about protecting the wealth of a modern nuclear family. The *oikos* known in the first-century world of Jesus was a household comprising servants, slaves, distant relatives, perhaps a tutor for the children and other workers. The *oikos* was, in other words, a small social unit that transcended biological family relations. The *oikos* cared for the poor and for the destitute; it cared for its members. As did the church later.

Economic intentionality can be highly focused and immensely productive. But sometimes, values and 'soft' forms of valuable social capital come out of time and space that might at first sight seem 'unproductive'. This is a subtle concept to grasp. In chapter 4, I mentioned Abby Day's prescient study of 'Generation A' women who, born in the 1920s and 1930s, have provided the backbone to organisations such as the Mother's Union.[30] Day's analysis picks up on the function of these lay-women in churches who are often found providing support through 'soft' forms of pastoral care and, in particular, through their catering. Specifically, she writes about them baking together.

As we noted in chapter 4 Day shows how through activities such as communal baking – which are technically uneconomic – nonetheless provid an environment that promotes mutual care, flourishing, prayer and pastoral well-being. It is obviously cheaper to buy the cakes and buns at any supermarket. But the communal baking fosters something else. One cannot send the same message to a mother who has just lost a daughter, or to a daughter who has lost a mother to breast cancer, with a box of muffins from the local supermarket.

The manifest intention of the communal baking is to provide a supportive catering service to the church and community. The latent intent that emerges is the thick pastoral care that the gatherings engender, which also produce deeper and richer spiritual lives. It makes no economic sense, please note, to bake goods like this. The value lies in the actual and apparent *inefficiency* – which leads to deeper, unintended rewards.

The early church had form on this count. It is a little-known fact that the Edict of Milan (AD313), which was an agreement between the emperors Licinius and Constantine to recognise the legal personality of churches, treated all religions equally, and as well as restoring lands and property confiscated under persecution, it made provision for donkeys. According to the agreement, Christians, calling on all others of good will, were to see that beasts of burden were not abused in transporting heavy loads uphill.

Such concerns may seem trivial to modern readers, but the Edict provided an early piece of evidence to support the view that the Christian faith had extensive interests in contributing to mutuality and social order – even in the minutiae of everyday life. Generations of Christians would follow suit on other issues where prevailing standards and social constructions of reality had to be undermined and cast aside if justice was to be done. The emancipation of slaves (William Wilberforce), equality for those sweltering under the yoke of oppression in America's deep south (Martin Luther King Jr) or the alleviation of poverty in Victorian London (William Booth) are but a few examples.

The Edict of Milan is widely regarded as the point at which the foundation for established Christianity was first laid, although the Edict did not establish Christianity in the formal sense. The emerging Constantinian settlement did, however, provide a paradigm that was to influence much of Europe as it embraced Christianity. This was to link civic governance, religion and the economy in the interests of providing sustainable patterns of social ordering that were of benefit to communities (e.g. the prohibition on usury). In England, for example, the relationship between a parish and its church was intrinsic to the identity of a place.

Communities that were economically and socially viable were able to sustain a church and the ministry born out of it, which in turn guaranteed a certain level of moral welfare, social improvement and pastoral provision (including the availability of the sacraments). Or, put another way, the very existence of a parish church within a community confirmed the identity of the place, conferring it with recognisable significance that invited a form of social ordering in which (among other things) the needs of the poor and other matters of moral concern could be addressed on behalf of the community. Churches were early agents of mutuality.

Similarly, the genesis of many hospitals, schools, hospices and other agencies for welfare (e.g. adoption and fostering) began their life as an extension of the pastoral provision of the church, intended for the common good. Throughout Christian history, there have been many movements and individuals whose faith has spawned something particular that has directly contributed to the reordering of society. Christianity has been especially prominent in healthcare, welfare and education, but has taken no less an interest in the moral well-being of society.

The global financial crises of the 21st century, with the collapse of major banks and the effective insolvency of countries in 2008 – Greece and Iceland come to mind – and the economic impact caused by Covid have prompted a new wave of ethical, economic introspection that is focused on the limits of capitalism in relation to the human condition and social flourishing.

In his work David Sainsbury reflects on the private equity bid for Sainsbury's, the family business that he once ran. In his view, the bid for the business was nothing more than an attempt to acquire the company, sell off the firm's property portfolio and take on additional debt in the process of acquisition (in much the same way that new wealthy owners of a Premier League football club might do). Sainsbury maintains that the bidders for his family business had no pretence of seeking to improve the performance of the company.[31]

The bid was, in other words, not about the flourishing of individuals, the company or the communities they serve. It was, rather, purely about profit for those driving the bid. In the face of this kind of dynamic, Sainsbury has become a staunch advocate of progressive capitalism. By this he does not mean to imply more state intervention, nor shrinking government and further deregulation. Rather, he means to infer better and more intelligent government that can be simultaneously nimble and strong, and, crucially, knows when to intervene and when to stand aside.

Sainsbury's reflections belong to a burgeoning genre of critical texts that have begun to cast some doubt on the implicit assumptions relating to the nature of humanity and society embedded in late capitalism. Sue Gerhardt, for example, writes as a psychotherapist and social commentator. In *The Selfish Society*, she muses on the consequences of a society focused on individual acquisition, independent of the concerns and needs of our neighbours and wider society: 'Selfishness is often a symptom of a failure of human connection.'[32] It is a failure of mutuality and our common life.

At issue here, perhaps, is the relationship between business, finance, social flourishing and morality. In Stephen Green's *Good Value*, he considers how capitalism, though obviously flawed, might take a wider account of spiritual and social needs.[33] For Green, who writes as both a banker (former Chair of HSBC) and an Anglican priest, the financial services industry has responsibilities to the people it serves.

Echoing Sainsbury, Green suggests that businesses have a duty to society that go beyond the creation of profit. While he acknowledges that 'open market capitalism' may be the best hope for creating wealth, this does not prescribe how individuals are to work together for the common good. This is especially so in an increasingly urban, connected and demanding world, where the intense and pluralistic pressures on morality and spirituality – which foster value and character in individuals and society – are threatened by the drive to individualistic self-improvement.

The nub of the problem with the current unchallenged dominance of capitalism within most developed-world socio-economic systems is that capitalism has become a kind of 'fundamental' of human existence. Theologians such as Kathryn Tanner have suggested that capitalism, as an outlook and philosophy, is something of a belief system.[34] It is almost as though God said, 'Let there be markets', and 'Lo, they were created, grew and multiplied.' Yet one should not simply read economics as a faux-religious creed. It can also be clothed in the rhetoric of 'hard science' – and indeed we note how the term 'political economy', a phrase which Marx and Engels would have understood – has been morphed into the simpler, apparently humbler 'economics'.

The consequences of this are serious, as 'economics' as a 'science' can then simply reduce everything to the realm of commodification: labour, services, relationships... and even religion. Drawing on the work of Michael Sandel, Rowan Williams singles out education as a sphere that is particularly under threat from commodification: 'That education could have some value other than improving profits seems to be unthinkable.'[35] Sandel himself thinks the balance may have tipped:

> We believe that civic duties should not be regarded as private property but should be viewed instead as public responsibilities. To outsource them is to demean them, to value them in the wrong way... without quite realizing it, without ever deciding to do so, we have drifted from *having* a market economy to *being* a market economy.[36]

Sandel is keen to prescribe the limits of the free market economy. We cannot 'buy' friends, for example, as friendship is constituted by certain norms, virtues and attitudes that are beyond pricing: sympathy, generosity, thoughtfulness and attentiveness cannot be replaced by market values.[37] To attempt to purchase such characteristics as commodities would be to simultaneously destroy them in the very act of procurement.

Money can't buy love, and it can't buy true friendship either. Yet the marketplace has an uncanny knack for developing and producing simulacrums that replace the slow, patient business of building relationships and developing reticulation with something that is quick and instantly gratifying. Richard Sennett's book *Together* cites the example of Phillipa, a teenager who has 639 friends on Facebook, and claims to know the vast majority of them. Sennett points out that if they each send a message to one another and then receive a response, that would be 816,642 messages to digest – simply impossible.[38]

Sennett is alive to the limits of capitalism and market economies. In a world where relationships are increasingly stretched by the demands of economic life, friendship, education, family life and love emerge as forms of social bonding and human flourishing that put the market economy back where it belongs: something that society has, rather than something that 'has' society.

As a final thought, let me turn to Alfred Idle (Nationwide's first mortgage customer in 1884). We talk a lot about building society today. Alfred Idle, when he had finished buying his house, carried on paying in to his building society – and watched with pleasure as it helped to create the first public library in his neighbourhood. Alfred's street was named after Walter Morrison, a strong supporter of housing reform and the cooperative movement.

Alfred was not alone. He was surrounded by like-minded people who were invested in the idea of self-improvement. His neighbours in the community included carpenters, clerks, factory workers and railway workers. A temperance society was set up and no pubs were allowed on the estate, to protect the community from gambling and alcoholism, which was rife at the time. Evening classes such as practical geometry, machine drawing and build construction were held, in connection with the South Kensington Science and Art department.

As a self-improver himself, Alfred was involved in the movement within his community. And Alfred got involved with other movements too. For example, take Charles Edward Mudie, a London bookseller who, in 1842, converted almost a third of his stock into a mostly non-fiction mobile lending library to help improve literacy for ordinary working people. Alfred moved out of London into the suburbs and began working as a librarian assistant at Mudie's circulating library. Mudie's library was influential in improving access to books in Victorian times. Indeed, Charles Darwin borrowed many books from the library as part of his own reading, and in turn the library bought hundreds of copies of *On the Origin of Species* to circulate to readers.

Alfred's support for the building society went beyond putting his savings there. He also went on to work for the society as an agent for Clapham, and his son (John Idle) was an agent for Wandsworth. He continued saving right up until his death in 1918, when he had £46 in his savings account.

Money and markets are not neutral in terms of their values. We are increasingly coming to see that the myopia of the market economy rests on a set of values and assumptions that prioritise the individual over the social, and wealth over wider concepts of flourishing. In calling government, business and financial services to account, the 21st century may yet see theologians playing a key and prophetic role in enabling society to see that what it might initially desire may not be what people actually need, and that tempting though wealth and individual autonomy may be, we are all connected. No one is an island.

Discussion questions

Beginnings: Stewards of kingdom currency

1 How does your church, fellowship group or congregation talk about money in order to:
   a Support the needs and upkeep of the church building, ministry, staff, clergy, etc?
   b Reach out to the needs of the local community – e.g. food banks, credit union, social work, charity shops, etc?
   c Impact the wider world for mission and ministry – including relief of the poor, refugees, asylum seekers, missionary agencies, healthcare projects, social and educational programmes, etc?

2 Does your church proactively fundraise, and if so, is this around a particular project, or a long-term commitment to a particular cause? How do we talk about our giving in spiritual, ethical and Christian terms?

Part 1: Mission, ministry, money

1 Two sides of the same coin

1 Is it helpful to distinguish between the things that belong to God, and those that are the property of the state?
2 When you read this gospel account, how else might you have answered the question put to Jesus?
3 How can we be faithful to the world and to God if we know that some of our taxes are allotted to arenas we might not support (e.g. military)?

2 Money magic

1 Does seeing Jesus as a taxpayer change your attitude to taxation and revenue?
2 How does your church or congregation raise the funds it needs to support its work?
3 Does your church raise funds for churches that cannot support themselves, and what kind of control might your congregation exercise over such giving?

3 Rewards and bonuses

1 The distribution of rewards and bonuses is uneven in the parables. In the labourers of the vineyard, all receive the same irrespective of their endeavour. In the parable of the talents, endeavour and entrepreneurship is intrinsically liked to rewards. Which parable do you prefer, and why?
2 What does the gospel teach us about our response to those inside and outside the faith who make no contribution to the life of the church?
3 Is it helpful to speak of heaven as a place of reward?

4 Economic miracles

1 The miracle at Cana is about patience leading to absurd abundance. How does this miracle, as a sign, point to one of the deeper themes in John's gospel?
2 'The biggest challenge facing the church… is coping with the overwhelming abundance and love of God' (Dan Hardy). What does this quote mean, and do you agree?
3 Why are so many of the miracles of Jesus focused on food and health, and what does this tell us today?

5 Crumbs of comfort

1 Many of Jesus' miracles are deliberately directed to the marginalised and ostracised of his day. What does this mean for our times?
2 The gospels record that Jesus seldom healed his friends or colleagues, and rarely ever people of significant social or religious standing. What does this tell us about 'kingdom currency' then, and now?
3 Try to put yourself in the shoes of the Syrophoenician (or Canaanite) woman. What makes her so desperate, and why does she persist?

6 Tax return

1 Why does the crowd react to Zacchaeus in the way that it does, and what does this tell us about Jesus' gesture?
2 Are there groups, communities or individuals in roles today that also earn social contempt and criticism? Would Jesus also eat with them today?
3 How do we, as a church, intentionally cross boundaries to heal social divisions and help restore a sense of common purpose in our communities and nation?

Interlude

1 Using the Ignatian Guidelines (see p. 168), invite each person in the group to act out a role in the parable: father, elder son, younger son, servants. If you have more in your group, the employer who took on the younger son as an indentured serf or slave is a character, as are the carousers who helped the younger son spend the money so prodigiously. You can also speculate on other roles – neighbours of the father, for example, or the unmentioned mother of the sons. What did they make of this story as it unfolded, and why did it end with both exuberant celebration along with deep, painful family bitterness?

2 In view of what we have said about Elton John's song and *The Wizard of Oz*, what is Jesus' parable trying to tell us about money, property, stewardship and grace?

3 What currencies are at work in the parable?

Part 2: Counting the cost

Part 2 (Counting the cost) offers an opportunity to wrestle with a more unusual thematic approach to Lent, Holy Week and Easter. Drawing on the Ignatian approach outlined (see p. 168), readers are invited to think through and reflect on the following questions:

7 Bureau de change

1 Where in our local midst do we find economic exploitation of the poor, powerless or gullible?

2 What emotions does this story evoke in us towards those who are exploited, those who perpetrate it, and the culture that might reinforce that economy?

3 How do we channel our anger at injustice?

8 The price of oil

1 How do we respond to excessive generosity that, though richly significant, seems wasteful?

2 Did those who resented the lavishing gift poured out on Jesus have a fair point?

3 Where do our values on thrift and excess come from?

9   The currency of love

1   What does the currency of love look like for you?
2   If Jesus is the 'body language of God', what is our church's 'sign language', and where is it found?
3   How can we know and share God's kingdom currency?

10   Thirty pieces of silver

1   Have you ever been falsely accused or betrayed?
2   What does justice, forgiveness and restoration look like for your betrayer?
3   How can our churches own a ministry that has honesty and integrity concerning the abuses it has perpetrated?

11   Gambling the foot of the cross

1   Who are those gathered around the cross, and what costs are they paying by being present?
2   How do we account for the gambling at the foot of the cross, and are there modern parallels?
3   'The wages of sin is death' (Romans 6:23) – so what debts are being wiped out by this death on the cross?

12   Burial costs

1   Joseph of Arimathea's gift parallels the woman anointing Jesus at the house of Simon the Pharisee. What motivated their gifts? Why were they offered with such humanity, intimacy and lavish care?
2   How is honouring and respecting the dead – especially ones at the hands of violence, injustice and cruelty – an aspect of God's kingdom currency and life-giving?
3   'We believe in life before death' (Christian Aid): discuss what this means for our Easter faith.

Endings: Mutality and building society

1   'Our churches were only ever meant to be God's construction huts on some building site – for it is the Kingdom of God in the world that God is building' (Bishop John Robinson, adapted). Do you agree? And whether or not you do, what is God seeking to build in your community, and for whom?

Appendix I: Costing salvation – Ignatian exercises

These questions are just for starters, but they should help the discussions in group study commence. Try to make sure that the group is comfortable in continuing with an Ignatian approach, and the memories, emotions and reflections that may be summoned in each participant.

The suggested questions are rooted in the conviction that the storyline of the gospels, beginning with the ministry of Jesus through to Lent, Holy Week and Easter, is our story, too. How Jesus journeyed to Jerusalem, the kangaroo courts, betrayals and sufferings, and finding new life beyond death are lessons for us all. How the early church responded and adjusted to becoming the body of Christ is also part of our story. Let your imagination take you from the first century to the 21st century.

When reading a healing miracle from the gospels, try to focus on the following, giving perhaps 5–7 minutes for each section. You can also adapt this approach for some of the vivid human stories Jesus gives us in several parables.

Look at the story through the eyes of Jesus

- What implications are there for you in this healing?
- How far are you in control?
- What are the costs for you?
- What problems or obstacles do you face?
- What is the salvation you bring?

Look at the story through the eyes of those healed

- What are your motives?
- What actually happens to you?
- What contribution did you make to the process?
- What obstacles are there?
- Who caused them, and why?
- Did you get what you wanted?
- At what cost?
- What was required for healing to happen?

Look at the story from the perspective of third parties

- What is your role in the story?
- Why do you act as you do?
- What problems are caused by you?
- Is anyone threatened?
- Is anyone missing out?
- Do the actions have cost-related consequences for you?

Look at the gospel writer's perspective

- Why did you include this story?
- How is it useful to your church?
- Who are your readers identifying with?
- What is the story saying to you?
- What would it cost you to retell and relive this story?

Appendix II: Coins and currency in the New Testament

Our true citizenship is in God's kingdom, but Christians are still required to pay what is due to earthly powers. Paying taxes is part of the bedrock of obligations citizens or residents undertake for the services that enable any civilized society to function. Those services include the work of first responders (police, firefighters, medics, etc.) as well as the social welfare foundations put in place to ensure justice or aid for the poor, the aged, and others in need. Education and basic social amenities and utilities for all are also one of the fruits of taxation.

The Roman Empire – like many others before and after it, including the British Empire – was not governed primarily for the benefit of the common people. Yet even so, empires often provide social order, roads, water, policing, and sometimes relief for the poor. While we may not always agree on the range and depth of services our governments should provide, we know that our taxes are essential in providing for us and for those who cannot help themselves.

Some governments may have laws and practices that may violate Christian purposes and ethics, as was true of Rome in the first century. Governments or their employees may demand bribes, impose unethical rules and regulations, subject people to suffering and injustice, and use the taxes for purposes contrary to God's will.

As with taxes, Jesus does not demand that we resist every one of these abuses. We can't fight every battle. Instead, we must act strategically, always asking what the establishment of God's kingdom on earth will further. Obviously, people are the most important currencies in the gospels – especially those with nothing to their name, or who are benighted, persecuted and afflicted. God's business is human currency.

Divinity is currency too – abused by religious leaders in the time of Jesus, and subject to inflation and taxes. Jesus is free. Grace is free. God's love is free. This is the economy God asks us to wrestle with.

But there are other currencies too, and here we list the seven coins mentioned in the New Testament, which demonstrate just how international the economy in Israel–Palestine was in Jesus' time.

1) Lepton or 'widow's mite'

The *lepton* was a tiny bronze coin of relatively insignificant value, and is the coin Jesus valued most, as it represented all the widow possessed (see Mark 12:42; Luke 12:59; 21:2).

2) Drachma

An unusual coin of Christ's time, as the Roman *denarius* had long replaced the Seleucid (i.e. Greek silver coins). It has been thought that perhaps the coin (mentioned only in Luke 15:8) was a Cappadocian *drachma*, since these coins have been found in Palestine and were contemporary with Jesus' story of the woman and her lost coin. Jesus' reference seems to be to a Seleucid for a bride's dowry portion retained from a wedding. Such coins would be passed from mother to daughter and had great symbolic value. This might explain both the presence of a coin no longer in current circulation and the woman's desperation in going to such lengths to find it.

3) Didrachma

The *didrachma* and *tetradrachma* (a *stater*) were silver coins from the city of Tyre, used in the temple's business. *Staters* were equal to shekels, and because the Jews were forbidden to issue their own silver coins, they were forced to use coins from this merchant city. The coins bore the image of Baal. Money changers were on hand to render service, changing foreign currency into these Tyrian coins for a percentage. Judas was paid with 30 *staters*.

4) Tyre shekel, stater or tetradrachma

The Tyre shekel was Herod's only silver coin and originally minted in Tyre. When Herod the Great completed the temple in 18 BC [AD18], he needed direct control over the official temple tax shekel, so he transferred production of this most important coin to Jerusalem.

5) Quadrans

The *quadrans* was an Imperial Roman coin meant to circulate throughout the Empire. The size of a Canadian or US cent, the *quadrans* bore religious symbols. The King James Version renders this coin as a 'farthing' – an old English coin (see Matthew 5:26; Mark 12:42).

6) Assarius

The *assarius* was an Imperial Roman coin meant to circulate throughout the Empire. The *assarius* was larger than the *quadran* and usually pictured the emperor. As with the *quadrans*, the King James Version renders this coin as a 'farthing' (see Matthew 10:29; Luke 12:6).

7) Denarius

Mina(s) and talents are money terms used in the New Testament but they refer to weights of silver rather than coins. The *denarius* is the most referenced coin in the New Testament: 16 times. The *denarius* was a silver coin worth ten assarii. This is the coin rendered 'pence' and 'penny' in the King James Version. Civil taxes to Rome had to be paid in this coin. Pious Jews questioned the morality of such an act (see Matthew 18:28; 20:2, 9–10).

Appendix III: Additional online resources

For further exploration into some of the themes looked at in this book, please see the BRF Resources Hub at **brf.org.uk/resources**. Martyn Percy has supplied two additional resources available on the Resources Hub:

1 Reparation reconsidered: slavery legacy in the Church of England

This article explores the importance of reparations today, given the catastrophic legacy intensive slave-based agriculture has visited upon many former colonies. Hundreds of years on, the liability of slavery continues to be worked out in the ecology of the land, the diets of the inhabitants, and the education and opportunities for the ancestors of slaves. Far from being something merely regrettable from the past, the legacies of slavery are with us in the present day and will continue to shape the future.

2 What3Words? Go, make, disciples: clarifications

A significant number of churches in the developed world have struggled with declining attendance during the post-war era. Many leaders within historic Protestant denominations – and that includes the Church of England – have turned to a rhetoric of discipleship to try and offset this trend, in part seeking to explicitly incorporate the laity into the work of maintenance and mission. This article, as a discussion starter and position paper, explains why an appeal to discipleship is misconceived and explains what 'The great commission' (Matthew 28) was originally concerned with.

Notes

1   U.A Fanthorpe, 'Atlas' in *Safe as Houses* (Peterloo Poets, 1995), p. 62.
2   Julian of Norwich in James Bryan Smith and Richard J. Foster (eds.), *Devotional Classics: Selected readings for individuals and groups* (HarperSanFrancisco, 1993), p. 71.
3   Adrian Desmond and James Moore, *Darwin* (Penguin, 1991), p. 47.
4   C.H. Dodd, *The Parables of the Kingdom* (Fount Paperbacks, 1978), p. 16.
5   John Dolan, *The Independent Methodists: A history* (James Clarke & Co., 2005), p. 48.
6   Frederick W. Faber, 'There's a wideness in God's mercy' in *Hymns Ancient and Modern Revised* (Canterbury Press, 1981), p. 481.
7   Luzia Sutter Rehmann, *Rage in the Belly: Hunger in the New Testament* (Cascade Books, 2021).
8   Gavin Francis, *Intensive Care: A GP, a community and a pandemic* (Wellcome, 2021), p. 14.
9   Abby Day, *The Religious Lives of Older Laywomen: The last active Anglican generation* (Oxford University Press, 2017).
10 Mary Grey, *Redeeming the Dream* (SPCK, 1989), p. 51.
11 Rehmann, *Rage in the Belly*.
12 Martyn Percy et al, *The Spirit of Witness: liturgies, prayers, poems and sermons for dissenters* (Canterbury Press, 2023), p. 77.
13 Simon Schama, *Rembrandt's Eyes* (Alfred Knopf, 1999), p. 685.
14 Schama, *Rembrandt's Eyes*, p. 685.
15 Harvey Cox, *On Not Leaving It to the Snake* (SCM Press, 1968).
16 See Lytta Bassett, *Holy Anger: Jacob, Job, Jesus* (Continuum, 2007).
17 Nigel Biggar, 'On judgement, repentance and restoration', in Martyn Percy (ed.), *Untamed Gospel: Protests, poems, prose* (Canterbury Press, 2017).
18 Andrew Hudgins, *The Never-Ending* (Houghton Miffin Company, 1991), p. 13.
19 Kate Compston, in Jane Morley (ed.), *Bread of Tomorrow: Praying for the world's poor* (SPCK, 1992), pp. 51–52.

20 Elisabeth Moltmann-Wendel, *The Women Around Jesus* (Crossroad, 1990), p. 98.
21 Nicholas King, 'Stations of the Cross', **thinkingfaith.org/articles/20130326_1.htm**.
22 'The 17-year-old making films fun for deaf children', **feeds.bbci.co.uk/news/newsbeat-58972808**.
23 Julian of Norwich, in Richard J. Foster and James Bryan Smith (eds), *Devotional Classics: Selected readings for individuals and groups* (HarperSanFrancisco, 1993), p. 71.
24 Julian of Norwich, in Joan Chittister, *Light in the Darkness: New reflections on the Psalms for every day of the year* (Crossroad, 1998), pp. 131–32.
25 Emily Dickinson, *The Complete Poems of Emily Dickinson* (Little, Brown and Company, 1924), p. 54.
26 Julian of Norwich, *Revelations of Divine Love,* edited by Grace Warrack (Methuen, 1917), p. 202, updated to modern English.
27 On this, see Christian Goeschel, *Suicide in Nazi Germany* (Oxford University Press, 2009).
28 'Judas Restored' by Ann Lewin is © Ann Lewin, 2009. Published by Canterbury Press. Used by permission.
29 On this, see Michael Screech, *Laughter at the Foot of the Cross* (Routledge, 2000).
30 Day, *The Religious Lives of Older Laywomen*.
31 David Sainsbury, *Progressive Capitalism: How to achieve economic growth, liberty and social justice* (Biteback Publishing, 2013).
32 Sue Gerhardt, *The Selfish Society: How we all forgot to love one another and made money instead* (Simon and Schuster, 2010), p. 115.
33 Stephen Green, *Good Value: Reflections on money, morality an uncertain world* (Allen Lane, 2009). I also strongly recommend David McWilliams, *Money: A story of humanity* (Simon & Schuster, 2024).
34 Kathryn Tanner, 'Is capitalism a belief system?', *Anglican Theological Review*, Fall 92:4 (2010), pp. 617–35.
35 Rowan Williams, 'From Faust to Frankenstein: Markets alone should not determine our conception of what is desirable', *Prospect*, 23 April, 2012, p. 75.
36 Michael Sandel, *What Money Can't Buy: The moral limits of markets* (Allen Lane, 2012), p. 10.
37 Sandel, *What Money Can't Buy*, pp. 137–41.
38 Richard Sennett, *Together: The rituals, pleasures and politics of cooperation* (Allen Lane, 2012), p. 145.